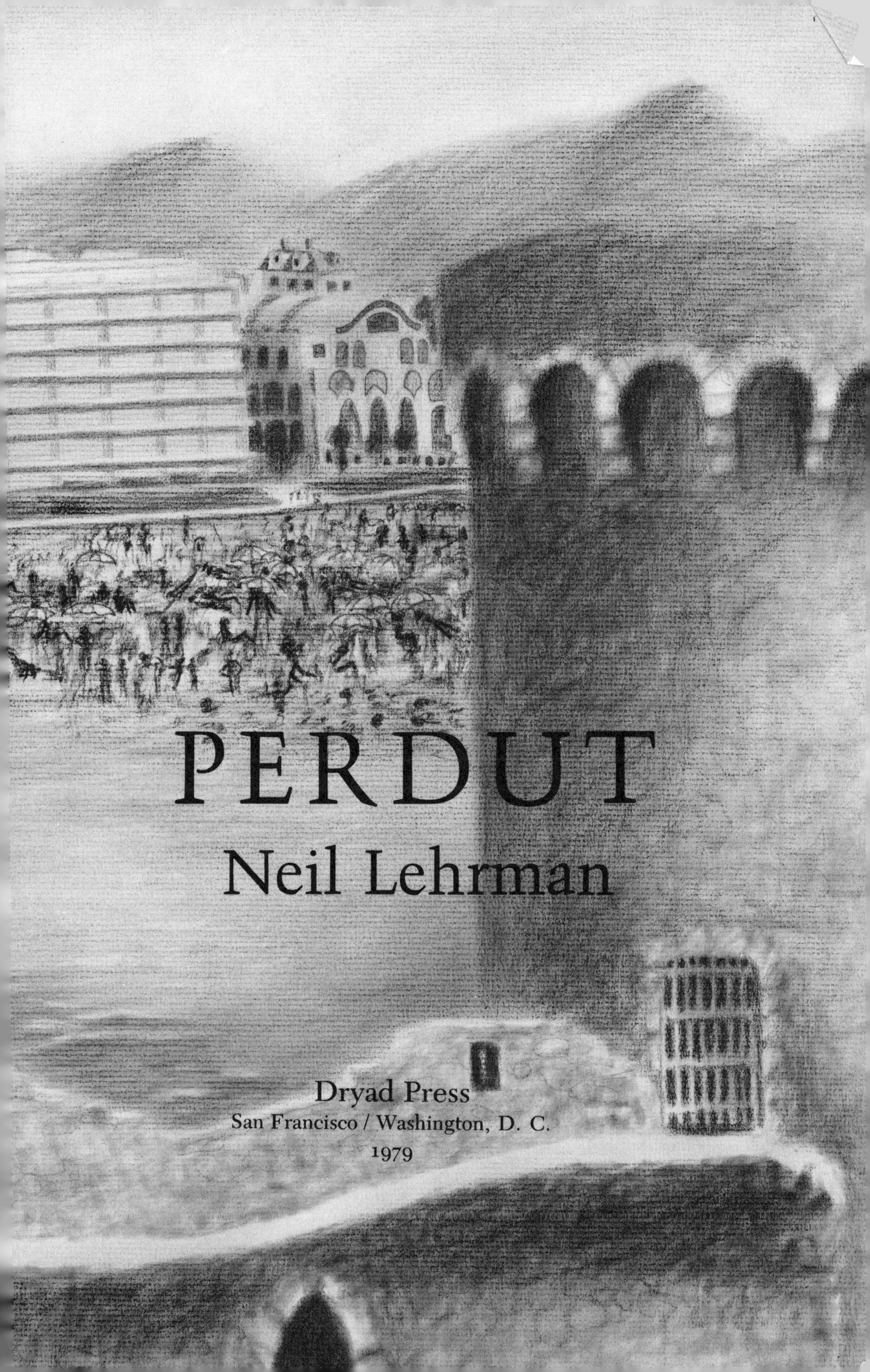

PERDUT

Neil Lehrman

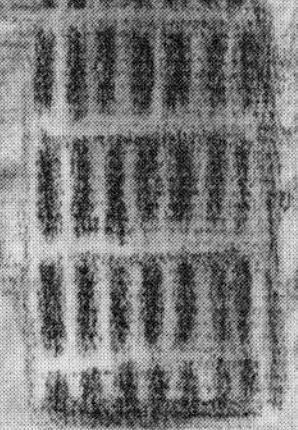

Dryad Press

San Francisco / Washington, D. C.

1979

ACKNOWLEDGEMENTS

Quotation on page 74 from the lyrics to "Proud Mary" by J. C. Fogerty, © 1968 Jondora Music, Berkeley, Calif. Used by Permission. All rights reserved.

Quotation on page 75 from the lyrics to "High Time We Went." Words & music by Chris Stainton & Joe Cocker, © Copyright 1971 Writers Workshop Ltd., London, England. TRO-ESSEX MUSIC INTERNATIONAL, INC., New York, controls all publication rights for the U.S.A. & Canada. Used by Permission.

Quotation on page 75 from the lyrics to "The last Time" by Mick Jagger/ Keith Richard, © copyright 1965 ABKCO Music, Inc. All rights reserved. International copyright secured. Reprinted by Permission.

This project is supported by a grant from the National Endowment for the Arts in Washington, D.C., a Federal Agency.

DRAWINGS BY: Manuel Fuentes
COVER PHOTO: Harald Stroh

Library of Congress Catalog Card Number: 78-20558
ISBN: 0-931848-22-9 (cloth cover)
0-931848-23-7 (paper cover)

FIRST PRINTING

DRYAD PRESS

P.O. Box 29161 Presidio
San Francisco, Ca.
94129

P.O. Box 1656
Washington, D.C.
20013

To the Memory of my Father and Mother,
Julius and Dorothy Lehrman

Perdut

Author's Note

As to places mentioned in this story, Tossa de Mar is a village on the Costa Brava of Spain. Though some of the other places mentioned do actually exist, there is no La Vida or Llibertat. All characters are fictitious with the exception of Max. He is, to my best recollection, exactly as I have portrayed him, and for all I know, still living in Tossa.

Neil Lehrman

1972

The Captain says I'll be in America before Christmas. He said it so proudly this morning and then gave me the bottle of whisky, as if the gift was supposed to soften the blow of the bad news. A week ago I was enjoying the winter in Barcelona, making plans to go to the Canaries for the holidays. And now it'll be America. America. The word sounds so strange, even though I've heard it all my life. You'd think I'd feel some excitement going back after all these years, but I don't. No one'll meet me at the dock. I can't even think of anyone I care for enough to telephone when I arrive. Except my kids. I'd like to see them, but how do you call after so many years without a word?

Brian had no one either. In that way we were the same, but in every other way we were different. I remember Raoul once telling me, "Pablo, you are very European, not American." I was never sure what he meant by that, but going home now I think I understand. Home? I only call it *home* because some more appropriate word escapes me. Brian, on the other hand, was very American, not European, and now he doesn't have to go home.

Sitting here with the tax-free whisky grating warmly on my throat for lack of ice, I keep thinking maybe I've been kidding myself right from the very beginning. I don't know. I don't know anything for sure anymore, except the whisky's just about gone, just like everything else.

It was only because Raoul was my friend and insisted the mayor buy La Vida, rather than expropriate it, that I was spared the humiliation of an official deportation. Not that I'm sure it really matters now, having been told never to come back to Spain. Never enjoy another freak summer in Tossa again. And for me, summer in Tossa was everything.

Why! "Why?" I begged Raoul as he drove me out of Tossa for the last time. "Why after all these years are they making me leave?" But my friend only kept his eyes fixed on the twisting coast road and, with the Spanish inflection betraying his English more than I could ever remember, said, "Pablo, it is because you are an outsider, even after all this time."

La Primavera

LA PRIMAVERA
(Spring)

I distinctly remember the sound of Brian's bike that first time. I remember it because you didn't find big 750's like his in Tossa. Brian roared into town at the end of one of those pleasant March days, the kind where the warmth breaks out around midday only to disappear again in the shadows of late afternoon. I was standing in the doorway of La Vida with nothing to do, having just opened the place up. Some of the town kids ran past kicking a tin can down the street and around the corner into the church plaza. From time to time their loud shouts would drift back over the buildings. But all in all, it was quiet, like it always was in Tossa that time of year, with the tourists gone and only the kids and stray dogs in the streets.

The noise of Brian's bike came from the Barcelona road. At first it was just an easy hum, like the buzz of a far-off chain saw, and then it came closer and closer, louder and louder until it was a roar in the next street over, chattering window panes and reverberating through the whole town every time he geared down at one of the blind intersections of the narrow streets. The angry whir whipped through the church plaza, wiping out the tin can game, and faded down the zigzag street to the beach.

Seeing the panorama of the white town bent around the cup-shaped cove and the old castle standing guard on the hill must've triggered something in Brian, for he opened the throttle to necksnapping speed and recklessly shot down the expanse of beach past the longboats and old women folding their green fishing nets. At the end of the promenade, he veered off the beach. The roar of the engine faded to a murmur as he wandered slowly through the senseless maze of streets in the old part of town. Then the engine came back to life again as he sped up at the sight of the familiar church plaza, this time turning toward La Vida.

From that first moment I saw Brian coming toward me, I was sure he was American. He had the regulation uniform of Levi's, sunglasses and a fatigue jacket flapping loosely against his hips. Close up I could make out the moustache and long hair looped in large curls, windblown from the ride. He stopped right next to me. The teardrop sunglasses hid all expression in his face.

"Open?" he asked, so softly I could barely hear him over the idling engine.

I nodded. He killed the engine and we went inside together. He took the seat near the coffee machine, laying his sunglasses on the bar. Without the glasses his whole face came alive. The blue eyes transfixed you like bullets. They weren't hard or cruel eyes, they just kept coming right at you, always penetrating.

"How about coffee?" he asked in the same soft voice that was just his normal tone.

I'd been by myself in Tossa for more than a month and was in the mood for small talk. "Where you headed?" I asked over the whir of the coffee grinder.

He waited for the machine to finish. "France, but it's too late to get much further today."

"Yeah, it still gets dark pretty early. Coming from Barcelona?"
He nodded.

"You didn't get far. It's only eighty kilometers," I said for no other reason than to keep the conversation going.

He mumbled something about oversleeping before the loud hiss of steam heating the milk for his coffee silenced us both.

"How long you been here?" he asked after a while.

That was the one question I hated because I would hear it all summer . . . but it was just spring and, after all, I was the one who wanted to talk. "Let's see . . ." I said while counting to myself, "More than eight years now . . . this is the start of the ninth. Longest time anywhere."

He looked through the window of the door. The kids were back, inspecting his motorcycle. "It's pretty quiet here," he said, turning back to me. "Is that why you stay?"

"Me, no. I stay for summer."

"Summer's that good here?"

"Hey, summer in Tossa's really freak!"

Looking back now I can't help but wonder if Brian's renting the tiny room on my roof terrace wasn't the crucial point of our friendship, the precise instant where a course change on the compass as slight as one second of one degree would have made all the difference. He decided on the cramped room the moment he saw it. He liked its snug feeling, with the stove and sink occupying virtually all the space not taken up by the bed or the monstrous wardrobe. It made no difference that the bed sagged, or that the mattress still had the winter dampness. He was too tired to care, and besides, it was only for one night, or two at the very most.

Maybe I'm making too much of all this with Brian. Perhaps I should be looking ahead, not brooding about the past. But Brian became such a big part of my life. No one had been that important to me in such a long time . . . maybe never! I must understand these strange feelings that keep coming over me. If he'd taken a room in some other pension, I think we'd still have been friends, but it wouldn't have been the same. Living over the bar like he did, we'd go on talking long after closing, the friendship building one night at a time.

Still, after all this time, I can't explain the mysterious quality that drew me to him. Brian was just different, even though he looked like so many others who wandered into Tossa every summer. There were his blue eyes, constantly reaching out, always demanding the esteemed part of yourself. And as if without choice, all of us gave. Those eyes! Always those eyes showing their gratitude . . . and the pain! He was such a baffling mixture of vulnerability and insensitivity with that arrogant bike of his. But the combination only seemed to make him that much more irresistable to us all, especially me.

When he first handed me his passport to register for the room, I saw his photo: no moustache and his hair so short and neatly combed that his incisive blue gaze was reduced to a daydream. "Brian McCabe," I read aloud from the info page, seeing he had written no name in the space for who to contact in case of emergency. I wondered if it was just an oversight. He was so young to have no one else, either.

I introduced myself. His handshake was firm, but you sensed a hesitancy like he was holding back some vital part of himself. At the time, I thought it was only his distraction while sizing me up, taking in for the first time my weatherbeaten face that Dominique had once described as sexy, like leather because it got better with age.

Her comment had made Brian laugh, and he told her with a

lying wink to me, "I only see a middle-aged cynic with deep-set eyes whose only turn-on for the girls is a mashed-in nose."

Dominique didn't realize he was teasing. "*Non, non!* Paul is beautiful because he always looks to be outside," she protested in her heavily accented English that sounded so freak only because she was French.

When Brian and I came downstairs from seeing the room, Max showed up like he usually did when it began getting dark. The King of Tossa trotted right through the partly opened door and settled down out of sight in his special corner at the far end of the bar. I poured a *cacao* into a clean ashtray and the old hustler was lapping away at the makeshift bowl before it touched the floor. He finished the drink in a flash and looked up with an unmistakable "well-where-are-the-seconds" look.

"No more," I said, waving him back to his corner. "You know, only one to a customer."

Now the old honcho used his most deliberate walk to get back to his corner, flaunting at its best angle his protruding ribcage from the off-season living in Tossa, and the mean-looking scratch on his flank acquired in some battle in the woods. At the far end of the bar Max made the turn to face us, as wearily and slowly as possible. The King of Tossa was in fine form for Brian's sake. Now he went into the best part of his act: pushing his front paws out in a long stretch, like he was getting the arthritis out of his joints. And then, with his bony ass still high in the air, he sank slowly to the floor, resting his head on his paws in cautious sleep.

"He yours?" Brian asked with eager interest.

"No, just a stray."

"Give him another on me."

Through half-opened eyes, Max was smugly watching Brian as he picked up the ashtray. *The stretch never failed on the new ones.*

"Hey, you don't want to give him too much," I said. "He'll follow you around the whole time you're here. Everybody will think he's yours."

"So what?" Brian asked in genuine astonishment.

"They'll hold you responsible for what he does, like when he knocks over the garbage cans or makes too much noise at night."

That didn't change Brian's mind. I handed him the bottle of *cacao*. "You give it to him. It's bad enough he's here all the time," I grumbled halfheartedly.

Max was up at the sound of the first gurgle, lapping away at his prize before Brian could empty the bottle into the ashtray. He finished faster this time, going back to his corner without the theatrical anguish of before.

The King of Tossa didn't even bother to open his eyes when I went over to comb through his coat for ticks and burrs. The bar was one of the few places he could enjoy unguarded sleep for the time being. In summer the tourists push him out of his corner, and the noise and crowds get so heavy he won't come around much. Still, summer's the best time for Max. The bony ribcage is buried under a coat of shiny brown fur, and the floppy ears bounce in time to his proud gait as he trots through the streets, all fat and handsome, coolly checking out the tourists for his next meal or a place to sleep.

I can't conceive of Max growing old. Of being tired and aching, haggard from the heat, or slowly going blind and dying. For me he'll always be the same, carefree and idle like summer in Tossa, following along behind you until a better thing comes along. Come to think of it, maybe I really dig Max so much because we're both the same, making it through winter off our summer fat.

Catalan chicks are so freak! The best fox show in the whole world is sitting on the Ramblas in Barcelona watching those long haunches walk past.

But the most mind-blowing Catalan fox of all was in Tossa. Nuria. In the subtle orange light of the Llibertat, every ounce of her slender nineteen-year-old body was prime cut, right down to the perfectly curved shoulder blades.

I took Brian over to the Llibertat that first night to see this supreme work of fox art, who was besides everything else, half French too.

Nuria, examining her fingernails, looked up when the door rattled and opened.

"Hello." The greeting in her melancholic lilt was a beautiful blend of French, Spanish, and English. You seemed to be hearing each separate language and yet none of them.

Her mother Madeleine was at her usual place, the last stool at the far end of the bar. She didn't even blink when we entered. She just went on staring at the coffee and cognac in front of her.

We took seats near the front door.

I was in a mischievous mood. "*¡Hola!* Madeleine," I called, just to annoy her.

She only gave me back a bothersome nod, like always, but I didn't care. I forgave the old hen everything because she was French. The French women are the Ultimate Foxes, always getting the most out of whatever beauty they have and keeping it together even in old age. Madeleine had weathered the years quite well. Her skin was still tight under the chin. And while I don't think she was ever beautiful, because of a hawk nose and wide eyes that spoiled her thin face, she was invested with a self-possessed majesty that made you understand why a proud Spaniard like Nuria's father would marry a Frenchwoman.

In the orange light, Nuria's scarlet sweater darkened to the color of dried blood. I leaned across the bar, leering right into those slanting, dark Asian eyes and whispered, "You look foxy as ever."

"He talks crazy," she said to Brian with a shrug, taking a drag on her Ducado.

We watched Nuria head down the bar for the nearest ashtray. When Nuria moved, she didn't walk, she floated.

"Isn't she freak?" I said.

"No trouble from her mother?" Brian asked. "I thought in Spain you don't come on so strong."

"Madeleine doesn't speak English, and anyway it's all eye-play and words—just a game between us. That's why I think Nuria enjoys it so much. We're like two kids together. It sounds sick but I really dig it. Something to do during the winter. In summer when the foxes are everywhere, I don't even think of her."

Nuria was back. "*Dos cervezas, por favor,*" I said. She took two beers from the ice box and opened them with the church key in the European style, bending her wrist downward.

"What does Llibertat mean?" Brian asked her.

"It is Catalan for, how you say . . ."

"Freedom," I said.

"Why not the Spanish word?" Brian asked.

"Because I am Catalan," Nuria said proudly in clipped, accented English. "Now there is nobody in Tossa . . . except he," she told me, meaning Brian.

"George is around somewhere."

"George, he is crazy too," she sniffed with indifference.

"Nuria thinks all of Tossa's crazy, right?" I said.

"Yes . . ." Her freak lilt stretched the word to almost two syllables.

The sound of scratching glass came from behind us. Max was looking at us through the bottom pane of the French doors.

"He always knows where you're at," Brian said with a laugh. "Do we let him in?"

When Brian opened the door, Max went straight for the fireplace in the back room. Nuria opened a *cacao*. She called and the King of Tossa came back, his wagging stub of a tail chopping up the air. Madeleine finished her cognac. She circled Max and started up the stairs, muttering something in French.

When Max finished, he licked his whiskers and yawned as Nuria petted him. Then he went back to the fireplace. The King of Tossa had his pad for tonight.

"Nuria, I think you like Max best of anyone in Tossa," I teased.

"Is because he is the only one not crazy. He all times shows the truth."

"You mean everyone else is a hypocrite, but you always know why Max does everything," Brian said.

"I no understand. You speak more slowly, please."

I translated.

Nuria nodded her understanding. "Yes, all the people is how you say . . ."

"Hypocrite," Brian said.

"In Tossa all times the peoples makes the money now. Now some peoples is very rich." She rubbed her thumb and forefinger together. "Because Tossa is little, all the peoples know each other much times. They afraid each talks different to he than to the other peoples."

"You like Tossa?" Brian asked.

"It is my home. I am Catalan. Now *Catalunya* needs all Catalans." She said it with such fierceness it ended the conversation.

Nuria's cousins Marcello and Santiago came into the bar. Marcello looked like he'd been closing every bar in town. He staggered across the room with a list that successfully defied gravity only because his squat body was built so close to the ground. Santiago followed his brother, saying hello for the both of them. His perpetual five o'clock shadow give him a vicious look that was a perfect match for Marcello's bull-like body.

"The Tossa Mafiosi," I whispered to Brian after Nuria went to join the pair at the far end of the bar.

The three were quickly immersed in Catalan conversation, dividing the Llibertat into two worlds. While I speak Spanish, I can only understand occasional words in Catalan. The language is a blend of French and Spanish, like *merci* and *gracias* becoming *merces*, or *buenas noches* and *bonne nuit* becoming *bona nit*. But the sound of Catalan has the beauty of neither; not the pleasing, smooth nasal tones of French nor the wingbeat *macho* rhythm of Spanish.

"Look at her!" Brian suddenly said. "Nuria's a different person with them."

Giggling at whatever Santiago had said, she was not the somber, stiff girl who had to concentrate on her English. She went on laughing for the longest time, clapping and jumping up and down like a little kid.

Brian and I watched, both feeling left out.

"When you going back to the States?" I asked.

Brian brushed the beer foam from his moustache. "I don't know. There's nothing I want back there. How long since you've been back?"

"So long I don't remember."

"You ever think of going back?"

"Me? No. Everything I want is here."

"It must be good to have a bar like La Vida."

"It's all right. I make enough in summer to not have to work the rest of the year. So I travel around."

"I didn't mean it like that. I mean it must be good to have something that stands for who you are."

"That's just a crock of shit. The place comes down one day and nobody notices. . . ."

"Except you."

"So what. You think anyone's interested? Everyone's only interested in their own trips. All that ever brings us together is balling. Everything else you do is only yours . . ."

"But doing it is enough!" he protested so seriously for his young years that I was jolted out of the temptation to continue baiting him.

"Hey," I said gently, "when I was young I also used to think that too, but later on when the dreams don't work out—"

"The trouble is," Brian cut in, "I feel that way now."

That put me off for a few seconds. I took a long sip of my beer. "You think you'll stay in Tossa for the summer?" I asked, to change the subject. All that existential crap didn't amount to flea shit. "There'll be plenty of work for the summer."

"Money isn't a problem. I'm cool that way."

"Sounds like you have it made."

"Some people would see it that way, but what the hell is the sense of it if you can't find something to make everything as big as it really is? You know, the poor are better off. They spend so much time fighting to survive, they never think about what would really make them happy." His blue eyes went taut as if someone had pulled hard on a string inside his head. "That girl down there is luckier than either of us, Paul. She has the passion. I don't know what it is exactly, but it's always grabbing you. Just look how alive she is. She may never leave this little place, but her life is far richer than mine."

I didn't know how to answer that, so I said nothing, becoming aware of the distinctive roar of George's Mini rattling the windows as the car climbed the hill to the Llibertat. "Forget Nuria," I went on after George had gunned the last dying revs out of the engine. "If the Tossa Mafiosi down there weren't too smashed to notice, they'd skewer you right up the old arse just for that look in your eyes. The Spanish don't dig us poaching their local game."

"Well, I don't suppose it would be very interesting anyway. The woman I want is at *that* end of the bar."

"There'll be plenty of foxes soon. Wait for summer," I consoled him, and broke out in a big grin at the very thought of it myself.

The front door opened and George boomed from the open doorway, "How's the whisky situation, Nuria?" With his straw sombrero, his moustache, dark complexion and pudgy build, he looked like the stereotyped Mexican of the old westerns.

He put his hat on the bar. Without the sombrero, his kinky hair emphasized his pear-shaped body. Nuria poured him a full measure of D.Y.C.

"George, you got your gun tonight?" I asked, ready to split if he did. Sometimes he'd get so drunk I'd have to throw him out of La Vida when he'd start flashing that pistol or a knife to prove to some tourist he was a CIA agent, which everyone in Tossa knew was a crock of shit. That night he didn't have the gun. Strangely enough, there weren't even any of the spy stories for a newcomer like Brian. George was oblivious to everything, except losing his girl Gloria. He started on it again, telling how she'd left him in Belgium for some German. The story was the same every time I'd heard it. I switched off inside, appearing to listen.

Suddenly George wasn't saying much. His eyelids were drooping, but Gloria's name was still perched on his lips, ready to burst out without warning.

"Daytime's always easier, George. Go sleep it off," I said.

For once he agreed. He pulled out his usual fat wad of pesetas and paid for all our drinks.

The door didn't shut completely after him, but nobody could be bothered to close it. We could hear the closing click of George's car door and then the engine roaring to life, completely destroying the night's silence.

"Now, *La Guardia* comes for sure," Nuria said disgustedly as she dropped George's tip into the *bote*.

By now Marcello was completely smashed. He'd managed somehow to get one shoe off, and was waving it while he yelled in Catalan. Nuria put her finger to her lips, pointing upstairs to where Madeleine was sleeping. Marcello's face crinkled into a drunken grin. He began hammering the bar with the shoe. Finally Nuria got it away from him. He tried to get it back, but she was too quick. He missed again on the second lunge and she tossed it through the open door.

For some reason the three of them found this all very funny. They were laughing like little kids while Marcello hobbled after his shoe, one shoe on, one shoe off. He came back like some retriever with a fetched bone and was pounding the bar again. Nuria grabbed for the shoe a couple of times, but this time Marcello was the quick one. Finally, her feint threw him off guard and she had it. And so the game began again. Marcello kept after the lure, homing in on his target until he was close, but then Nuria hurled it at the door again. No sooner had the shoe whistled past me than I heard the crash of shattering glass. Everything went quiet.

The three of them put their hands over their mouths to muffle new spurts of laughter. From upstairs came Madeleine's scolding, but the force of her anger was lost on me because it was in French. Nothing can sound ugly in that language.

Nuria went to the steps. Whatever she said soothed Madeleine into silence. Marcello limped over to retrieve his shoe. I heard the tinkling of the glass as he picked it up, but then none of the other expected sounds followed. I turned to see why Marcello hadn't moved.

Two *Guardia* soldiers stood in the doorway; their patent leather hats gleamed like miner's lamps in the orange light. You rarely see the *Guardia Civil* in the daytime; like bats, they usually come out at night, standing in darkened doorways as still and upright as they can, peering over the drawn-up collars of their capes and saying nothing to you if you should happen by.

Once in La Vida, a little too drunk to care, Raoul told me, "Ah, Pablo, the *Guardia* will not be happy until they have a man to watch every doorway in Spain. Only then can the government be truly secure."

"But who'll watch the *Guardia?*" I slurred, also too drunk to care.

"One problem at a time, my friend. We Spanish try not to think too far ahead." He held his glass up to the light with a broad grin. "It spoils the drink."

In the Llibertat came the silence that follows the *Guardia* everywhere, the silence that is either challenge or fear. The two intruders, as identical with their beardless faces and their uniforms as toy soldiers, waited for one of us to speak. But everyone, even Brian, instinctively knew better. Finally the thinner soldier gave in. "What is happening here?" he asked in stern Spanish.

"Nothing," Nuria answered curtly, also in Spanish.

"Do not tell me nothing. I have ears," he barked and dropped his eyes to the broken glass at his feet.

"An accident," she said coolly, coming around the bar with a dustpan. She waited beside Santiago, the impatient expression on her face implying their departure would clean up the glass . . . and the problem.

"Only an accident," the thin one snorted defensively. The worst thing of all that could happen to a Spaniard was happening to him—losing his sense of *machismo* in front of a woman, and a nineteen-year-old girl, at that.

The shorter and heavier guard inspected Brian and me. "*¿Pasaporte?*" he ordered stiffly. His jaw movements had worked his hat to a slight tilt. It made him look silly, but he refused to give us the satisfaction of adjusting it.

"I do not have it with me," I said, hating my obsequious Spanish tone.

He turned to Brian, who had watched all of this without any flicker of expression. "*¿Pasaporte?*" he asked again, a little more defiantly. Brian shook his head and tapped his pocket to mean he didn't have it either.

"Where do you sleep?" he asked in Spanish.

"La Vida," I answered for him.

"Bring them to the office tomorrow!" the guard ordered, more harshly than necessary.

"What for!" I snapped back. "You're acquainted with me. I've lived in Tossa for a long time and he's only a tourist leaving soon."

Max's quick bark shot around the room before the guard could answer. The King of Tossa was in the archway behind us, thrusting out the white blaze on his chest like a royal mantle. What had got into the old honcho showing off like this? It was crazy! He'd been around long enough to know better than hassle the *Guardia* with nowhere to run. All I can figure is Max thought that with Brian there nothing could happen. Max was always crazy-brave with tourists nearby because he knew the Spanish never do anything then.

Now it was all becoming a dream. Max's next bark echoed fiercely on the stone walls and spooked the thinner soldier so much he stepped back. I could see his arm dropping, the black holster opening, the pistol appearing like a snake coming out of its hole, daring us to pursue our defiance now. Somehow I wasn't scared yet. I was seeing this like it wasn't happening here, but somewhere else, on a movie screen or a television.

"Whose dog is he? If he barks again I will shoot him," the guard commanded, pointing the gun at Max for emphasis.

"Whose dog is he?" the *Guardia* repeated.

We were all stock still. Breathing seemed unnecessary. I prayed the silence wouldn't let Max think he was winning this game, and bark again. We could all hear Madeleine coming downstairs, muttering in French until she reached the last few steps where she could see the *Guardia*. "*¿Qué pasa?*" She shifted into Spanish with no sign in her voice of surprise or panic.

"There is much noise here," the gun-waving *Guardia* said, moving his mouth very little. "Whose dog is this? He is a nuisance. If he barks once more . . ." He pointed the pistol squarely at Max again.

"He belongs to no one, but he has many friends here," Madeleine said, approaching Max. Her calm seemed to relax the man, for he lowered the pistol. Seeing the initiative was now hers, Madeleine went on firmly, "You do not shoot firearms in my bar."

"Keep him silent," the *Guardia* grumbled while putting away his gun.

"Santiago. *Un cacao,*" Madeleine ordered, pointing to the ice-box. Santiago handed her the bottle. She moved toward the staircase, calling to Max, and he ran up the steps after her.

Marcello, who was still holding his shoe, dropped it on the floor and pushed his foot into it while muttering to himself in Catalan.

The guard with the tilted hat snarled, "You wish to talk, you speak Spanish—not Catalan."

Marcello spat out more words in the prideful Catalan, his face getting red. The *Guardia* moved a step closer, finally adjusting his hat. "This is Spain. You speak Spanish!"

Santiago came out from behind the bar. I think he was afraid Marcello might go for my beer bottle, for he stood between Marcello and the bar. He placed his arm amiably on his brother's shoulders. "You see he is drunk. Nothing has happened here. Just too much wine," he explained with a generous smile.

Nuria came forward to provide a greater show of strength. "Do you wish a drink? If not, please leave. I wish to close."

"No drink," the thin one growled, casting his eyes down again to the broken glass as if to have the last word on the matter. Then he turned to Brian and me. "Remember, bring your passports tomorrow morning," he commanded severely, to salvage their only victory of the night.

Nuria closed the door after them and began sweeping the glass into the dustpan.

"That crazy pig pulled a gun. Can you believe it!" Brian hissed. "We haven't got trouble, have we?"

"I think is no problem. Only *normal*," Nuria assured him.

Santiago came over. "I am sorry for the problem we make for you. They are bad."

Brian shrugged it off. "It's ok."

Santiago gave a relieved grin. "I pay you a drink."

"Tomorrow. It is late. I close," Nuria said.

They couldn't have picked a more perfect site for *Guardia Civil* Headquarters than the narrow street off the church plaza that got hardly any sun all day. The crisp chill of the shadows only added to the general terror of the place where all the green bats hid in the daytime. Inside the old building was even worse. The thick gray walls held the winter so well that in March it was cold and wet as December, and it would remain that way well into July before the steady heat of summer could finally drive out the dampness.

A carbon copy of the *Guardia* soldiers from the night before showed us into Raoul's office. Raoul was seated at his desk with his jacket on. Poor Raoul! Even in full uniform he couldn't be foreboding. He was slender with the fairest skin I ever saw on a Spaniard.

When Raoul saw me, he stood up and extended his hand.

"Pablo, you are here? How good." He always spoke English to give our friendship a naturalness his job wouldn't allow, and, I suspect, also to minimize eavesdropping. "I think this is the first time you are in my office in all the years, eh Pablo?" He liked using the Spanish derivative of my name, for it gave us a sense of intimacy.

"It's business, I'm afraid," I said quite formally. "Two of your men ordered us last night to bring our passports to your office."

"Why?"

"There was some noise at the Llibertat. They came to investigate. They almost had a run-in with Marcello."

Raoul brushed back the loose strands of his graying widow's peak. "Again! He and Santiago are always in trouble. A constant irritation to my men." He looked thoughtfully past us to the empty doorway. "Well, they are too old for me to talk to their family, and to bring them here is a waste of time. . . . There are more important things now."

"Do you know one of your heroes pulled out his gun because Max barked at him?"

"I am sorry, Pablo." He gave Brian a plaintive glance to include the stranger in the apology. "My men are nervous. Yesterday another *grupúsculo* exploded a bomb. Two people are dead. They call themselves revolutionaries; they are nothing but murderers!" he said angrily before catching himself. "They may pass through Tossa. It is believed they will try to cross into France."

"There was nothing in the papers or on television," I said.

"Pablo, it never is." A self-explanatory grin washed across his pale face.

"Do you really think they'll come here?"

"The world never comes to Tossa," he explained, as if it were a well-known fact.

"What a pity," I said caustically.

Raoul was annoyed with my sarcasm. "Please do not start that again, Pablo. You know I am not ambitious."

It was just like the *Guardia* to have one of their few intelligent officers, who had also been to college in the States, commanding the garrison of a fishing village where the most serious crime was smuggling in Japanese radios via the beach at Cala Salions.

"Who are you?" Raoul said to Brian, his tone growing official again.

Brian handed over his passport.

"You stay in Tossa long?" he asked while leafing through the pages.

"I'm leaving soon."

"You have money?"

"Yes."

"Good." Raoul smiled, content with the expected answer. "You are the one with the large motorcycle, no?"

"Yes . . . how did you know?" Brian's face showed his surprise.

"As you Americans say: I'm paid to know, *Señor* . . ." he looked to the front page of the passport for the name, "McCabe." His small smile broadened as he handed the passport back, saying in a more friendly voice, "It is a small town, *Señor* McCabe. My only request is that you try to run your motorcycle quietly, especially at night."

"No problem," Brian said in matching friendliness.

"I will see you for chess soon, Pablo. Do you play chess, *Señor* McCabe?"

"A little."

"Well then, perhaps a game before you leave Tossa. It is great exercise for the mind," Raoul said with mild interest as we turned to leave.

Summer in Tossa's really freak, but I think I loved the spring most of all because each day's a little longer than the last and the weather a little better. And best of all, summer's still to come!

Like a caterpillar sensing the coming season, Tossa slowly wriggles out of its cocoon in the spring. All the doors and windows are flung wide open to flush out the winter, and all along the streets the whitewash comes off the store windows. The optimistic smell of fresh paint is everywhere, giving me a high like when I was young and flush with the faultless confidence of youth and I thought there was no fox, no gig, nothing that couldn't be mine if I really wanted it.

The "tomorrow" for Brian to leave Tossa never came. On the sunny days we'd go down to the beach to work on our tans. We were the only sunbathers stretched out on the pebbled sand, now cleansed of all its trash by the winter storms. Tossa was growing on Brian. Once, while we sat on the beach, he said, "When I was in Nam, there was always this feeling if I could just go to sleep, the fear would go away and I'd wake up someplace good. That place was just a feeling, nothing I could ever describe, but it was Tossa. I know now it was!"

The vagueness that always precedes tears appeared in his eyes. I wanted to say something, anything so he wouldn't be left there so naked. It should've been something important—about me— something we could've shared, but I was stopped up like some constipated sinner in church, too scared to confess his worst deeds. All that I could bring myself to talk about was the night of my first summer in Tossa when I had to hide from the *Guardia* behind some fishing boats right in the middle of balling this Dutch fox with both of us drunk and sandy-assed naked, trying to be quiet as the moon.

My God! Has my life shrivelled to such meaningless trivia! Maybe I should've tried telling Brian that fear wasn't only with you on night patrols. Fear was having made the decision at thirty to leave everything and always wondering down deep inside yourself if it was the right choice, even when it didn't matter anymore because it was too late to go back.

Brian, even Big Ben, were taking steps that summer I'm not sure I could, even now, when there's nothing else to do. *All my life I've retreated from the edge!* Still, with Brian, I was closer to that big leap than with anyone. One night in an after-closing rap he'd said how he admired me giving it all up in the States for the life I wanted. It didn't matter to him I'd run out on the responsibilities of my kids or family. "You've lived without compromise," he assured me. "Don't you see the strength in that identity is the greatest thing you can give anyone?"

"But what happens if the life you've abandoned everything for doesn't work out so well?" I blurted out before I realized what I was saying.

"Paul," he said, pretending not to notice my uncharacteristic letdown, "good decisions are the ones you never regret making no matter how they turn out."

No sooner had Big Ben stepped off the Barcelona bus than he was on the beans again, strung out on uppers in the morning so he could do downers in the afternoon. You'd see him staggering from bar to bar like a drunken bear with goldfish eyes all bloated up from pills and wine. He had been like that since coming back from Holland, all decked out in his new Manchurian image, sporting the Fu Manchu moustache that braided into two long strands, with a small goatee as the final touch.

Ben had been around Tossa almost as many summers as me. He

didn't have to work, getting by on a small disability pension from the time he'd contracted polio in the Army. I liked Ben, but I wouldn't call us friends. Bar comrades was more like it. We always managed to keep the wall of saloon talk between us. The closest we ever came to anything intimate was his birthday a few years ago when I asked in one of those drink-in-hand, arm-around-the-shoulder moments how it felt to be forty. It was meant to be one of those questions where you don't expect a real answer. Just something to fill up those agonizing silences when all of a sudden you feel you don't belong where you are.

Ben's eyes couldn't fight off my question. They were too heavy with pills and booze to do anything but thicken in self-pitying exhaustion, like his voice had. "Christ, Paul, statistically I'm half-dead already."

The answer froze me. All I could think to do was finish my glass of champagne and be glad Brenda's walking up was my excuse to turn away.

Ben, Brian and I were in the Llibertat for a nightcap after I'd closed up. As usual, Ben was way ahead of us. The reds were doing the talking, rattling off fragments of unrelated monologues in the abrupt stops and starts of a poorly spliced tape. Ben lugged his immense, grizzly-bear body around to face us. "What do I do, you ask," he ranted softly, more to himself than us. "Watch the beach, that's what!" He held his hand up for dramatic effect. "What's wrong with watching the beach!"

He was flashing back for some incomprehensible reason on a conversation with Brian the first time they'd met. Now Ben was off on a new tack. "Stick around, Brian, summer in Tossa's for people like us . . . it's the only place we'll ever belong." He got up and shuffled along the bar with the slight limp left from his bout with polio. "Everyone needs some kind of glue . . . why . . . why does everyone need some kind of glue! I had all that baggage, Brian . . . can you dig it?" He slumped down on the bar stool near Nuria this time. "There I was with all the other suburban buffalo waiting for the 6:05. Blowing $5 a day on whisky! Nuria . . ." He leaned over the bar to make sure she heard him. "Another Estrella." But he left the barely poured beer to go back and paw Brian's shoulder. "How's our new citizen?"

"Ben, go home and get some sleep or we'll never make Barcelona tomorrow," Brian said, slipping gently out from under Ben's arm.

"Yeah, good idea." He was up off the chair. "All the baggage . . . the kids, the wife, the home . . . a nice home . . . did you know that? Shit, you fellows know I live on less than $5 a day right now . . . and it's not the same all the time like all them damn neons signs going on and off, on and off on the ceiling all night till you knew what color was next . . . what day . . . just left one day . . . left the firm without a word . . ." He was at the door now. "Watch yourself, Nuria . . . Paul's like Max around a bitch in heat," he chuckled, before lowering his head and reminiscing, "My daughter must be just about your age now, Nuria. And pretty too, but in a different way. Big-boned beauty . . ." You couldn't make out any of the rest of his hoarse mutterings. "*Bona nit*," he finally offered before closing the door.

"Why he does that all the time?" Nuria asked.

"A man's got to do something," Brian said, filling his glass from Ben's untouched beer.

Nuria only shrugged as she lit her cigarette. "He all times crazy. He haves no fire in him," she said, gesturing with the flaring match.

"You have plenty of fire," I leaned over the bar to touch her hand, ". . . for both you and me."

"You crazy too," she scolded, coolly pulling back. But there was a small smile on her lips as she shook out the match.

All of a sudden the French doors behind me were opening again.

"Finally fuckin' made it and who's 'ere to welcome us 'ome?"

I knew who it was before I turned around.

"'ey, Paul. 'ow the bleedin' 'ell are yeh?" Pete shouted.

"You bastard, you made it back!" And then I saw Terry right behind him. "And you too!" I pulled them into a hug, the three of us rocking back and forth in laughter.

Brenda came in behind them, breathless from the walk up the hill. "Yeh could bloody well wait a second for me."

She got the biggest hug. And a kiss. I took a step back, still holding her hands. "You look really freak."

"Lost two stone. I'm watchin' meself this year. No 'eavy drinkin.'" The pride of the accomplishment sparkled in her eyes. She was really foxy again in her snug slacks and a tight short-waisted olive jacket with large silver zippers on the pockets and sleeves. Her black hair had the brilliant sheen of crow's feathers in the soft orange light.

"What's this?" I laughed, holding up her hand with the green fingernails.

Her smile showed the missing tooth at the corner of her mouth. "It's the latest, don't yer fancy it?"

"It's still bloody cold at night 'ere," Pete moaned, rubbing his hands together. "We 'itched all night from Lloret but there ain't no fuckin' people on this cowin' road at night. We must'a walked 'alfway before some spic picked us up—"

"Whose fault was that?" Brenda scolded. "Yeh bleedin' drink too much. 'e wouldn't leave the bar. Terry and me, we 'ad to drag 'im out to the road."

"Fuckin' pissed worse than me that spic was! 'e drove like 'e was out of 'is bleedin' 'ead, all the time mind you, chattin' up Brenda with one 'and on the wheel and t'other 'and on 'er fuckin' leg!"

"Strokin' me like I was 'is cat or sumthin'," she added indignantly.

"Did you enjoy it?" I asked, knowing I was grinning like that cat.

She turned her angry glare on me.

Pete brushed his long hair from his eyes. "Aw, 'e was full of shit. All them spics are the bleedin' same. They fuckin' think that every bird down 'ere on 'oliday is waitin' to get their end away."

Brenda turned impatiently to Pete. "A lot of bloody good yeh were, just sittin' there in the back as nice as yeh please mumblin' 'give it plenty, babe.'"

"'ey, look. We were bloody lucky to get the ride. Otherwise, we'd be kippin' in some field now," Terry said in his dreamy way. The sunworshipper looked unnatural in his white skin and brown hair. A month from now his nonstop, ten-hour beach days would make him a chocolate-colored blond.

"Anyone else 'ere yet?" Terry asked.

"You're the first outside of Big Ben . . . and George, of course. Gloria split from him."

"We 'eard that in London from Phil. 'e's comin' back too."

"Yeh staying' long?" Terry asked Brian when I introduced them.

"Don't know. Whatever's cool."

"That's right," Pete agreed. "Make 'ay when the sun shines, luv when it rains, and life's a breeze."

"Nuria, give us a beer," beckoned Terry, sitting down at the bar.

"The same," Pete said. "I've got a right thirst on."

Pete took a long sip from his glass. "Bad as this spic beer is, it always tastes good in Tossa. The start of summer's always the best time," he crowed while looking around the bar.

"What'd you do when you left here?" I asked.

"Yeh remember that Aussie bird, Kate, who worked at Sivas? When we got to the border last fall I says, "Which way, luv?" And she points east and we're off. 'itched to India with fifty quid between us, we did. More than two fuckin' months, but we got there. Once we 'ad to stay seven days at this poxy crossroads in Afghanistan waitin' for a fuckin' ride. That were the only bad part. Kate took a boat to Sidney from Calcutta. She's not comin' back. I signed on a fuckin' steamer bound for Canada. Got off in Montreal with 500 quid in me pocket and bin dossin' ever since."

"That steamer were a bit of fuckin' luck," Terry reminded him.

"It bloody well was. I was skint. Down to me last penny. I would've sold me passport, but I done that once before. I reckon sumthin'll always come along to 'elp ol' Pete out." He gave us a triumphant grin before finishing the beer.

"How's Lloret? Brian and me keep meaning to go over."

"It's great," Pete said, looking around the empty room in contrast. "But two fuckin' weeks in that place is enough. It's all fish and chips with them old geezers. It's fuckin' Blackpool come to Spain, it is."

"As pissed as yeh was the whole time, 'ow'd yeh know?" Brenda bitched at him, but teasingly, like she wasn't mad anymore about the whole thing.

"You like Tossa?" Brian asked her.

"Bin comin' 'ere four years now. After that long yeh luv it. 'ow long yeh been 'ere?"

"Almost six weeks."

"Yeh fancy it now? I mean when it's like this?"

"It suits me. But I'm glad to see some people come. I'm ready for summer."

Those blue eyes were taking her in. She knew it and returned the attentive gaze. She had always preferred Americans, even me once, for a time.

"You going to work for Sivas again this summer?" I asked Pete.

"Unless sumthin's fucked up. Terry's for Bounty."

"Not me," Brenda said. "I've 'ad enough of them discotheques."

"Want to work at La Vida?"

"Maybe. I'll talk to yeh tomorrow." She was more interested in Brian. "Yeh gonna be 'ere the whole summer?"

"I think so."

"Yeh'll like it," she said warmly. "There's all kinds of interestin' people 'ere."

"You shouldn't have been in such a hurry to get here. It's still pretty dead. You're the first workers to arrive," Brian said.

"I weren't comin' so early but me girlfriend changed 'er mind, so I decided to catch the charter with Pete and Terry."

"You're just friends, nothing more?"

"No, nothin' more! We're just mates," she smiled, understanding at once.

Pete and Terry were intently telling me about their week-long drunk in Lloret. I could hear Brian and Brenda talking also, but I didn't really hear any of them. All I knew is I felt good. Summer was finally here. Sure, in a few months, working straight through seven nights a week, you'd hate the endlessness and the boredom of the same people. But for now it was good because it was green and new. And like I said, all still to come.

". . . And one day we're really pissed up in the Captain's Arms, when who walks in but Jimmy. I thought that fuckin' bloke was in Malfi! 'e's got some bird keepin' 'im, 'e 'as. A nice gearbox, she is. I wouldn't mind spearing 'er meself. Paul, we were pissed as a cunt that night. 'ave never been as fucked as I was that day . . ."

"What did you do in Lloret, beautiful? You get drunk all the time too?" I asked Brenda.

"Yeh know better than that." Her elliptical eyes squinted to balance her smile.

"'ey Paul, we 'ave to 'ave another of them beach bucket parties. I was never so paralytic in me life. Lost me bleedin' job at Charlie's. Too pissed to stand at the bar . . . yeh remember that Spanish bird with the big knockers and me not understandin' one fuckin' thing she's sayin'? And I ask yeh what the cunt wants. And yeh say 'you'! What a fuck she was!" he roared.

"How about a walk down to the beach?" Brian asked Brenda.

"Sure," she said.

I could see them through the French doors as Brian took her hand going down the porch steps.

"That bird's already got a new one," Pete chortled. He finished the last of his beer. "Another one, Nuria. Nuria looks great as ever, eh Paul?"

Nuria smiled evenly and took a long drag on her cigarette before getting the beer.

L'Estiu

L'ESTIU
(Summer)

*H*ey, summer in Tossa is really freak!

The warm, sunny days on the beach with all those beautiful foxes in bikinis trying to get their tans; everyone making the nightly rounds of the jammed bars and discotheques where the rock music was just another small voice in the drunken din; or just sitting at some cafe and watching the crowds and cars filling up the tiny streets to the point of bursting.

No, none of these images is really summer in Tossa for me. They're only the visible surfaces, like the picture postcards the tourists send home. They don't begin to touch what I really loved.

Brian once told me, "You know what makes this place so magical? You're sitting outside Bar Simon after a great day on the beach, feeling beautiful and tan with the fresh smell of salt water still on your skin. You see all these people walk by, and you know some of them, I mean really know them. You wave to them and they wave back. And it hits you this town is so small we only have each other."

I think that comes closer than anything else to why we all came back each year. There was an intimacy, an affection for each other that grew up out of the roaring days of summer. It was more than camaraderie—we were a family caring about each other. And while this caring was something you couldn't see, you knew it was there, like the air we breathe.

Each day you could see the summer tide rising as the packaged tours roll into the bus station. But it's never summer in Tossa for me until the Feast of Corpus Christi. The Catalans seem to celebrate this holiday a little more spectacularly than all the rest, as if it were their swan song until the next winter.

They pave the streets with flowers—a rainbow of purple and yellow and green petals as elegant as any float in the Rose Bowl parade. At six o'clock the procession starts from the church as it has for centuries, going back to when Catalonia was a nation. The priest comes through the great church door and the men follow, cupping their hands over the flames of their long candles. Then come the children. These same kids who usually run wildly up and down my street shattering the sedate afternoons now march in their Sunday best with serious faces, like well-disciplined soldiers going off to battle, as if in their own innocence they sense better than any of us this surrender of their world to the tourist summer.

I watched the parade this summer like every year and found myself, like all the other tourists, unable to take a step, even though the last kid had gone around the corner. It's always so spooky how so many could tread upon the flower arrangements without disturbing a petal. Someone in the crowd snapped a picture and the shutter click was a signal to the herd. We began milling around, breaking up the colored patterns under our feet.

In Spain on Corpus Christi Day, a bar can't open until the parade has passed its door. I poked my head in to tell Brenda she could serve now. She had her back to me, stretching on tiptoes to pour coffee beans into the grinder. The tight slacks hugged her trim little ass like a rubber glove.

"Hmm, that's very nice," I said, going inside.

She smiled over her shoulder. "Yeh're a cheeky one."

"Seen Brian?"

"'e's gone for a bit of a walk to clear 'is 'head, 'e said."

"He sick or something?"

Her hands went to her hips peevishly. "'ow would I know! 'e's none of m' bleedin' business anymore." She picked up the dish-cloth and started to dry the glasses with uncharacteristic thoroughness. "I never understand yeh bloody yanks," she muttered, giving the towel a final, vicious twist inside the glass.

"Paul, I'm going to work at Sivas," she blurted out through a long sigh, as if she'd finally been able to make up her mind.

"I thought you were tired of discotheques."

"Yeah, but 'e's always 'ere," she countered in a weak voice.

"He's always there too. It's a small town, Brenda."

"It's different, what with the noise and all."

"It's going to be a pain in the ass breaking in someone new, but if that's what you want. Who's looking for work?"

She perked up at the question. Making it so easy to quit was an unexpected boon.

"Bonnie says she'd like to work 'ere."

"Fine."

"No 'ard feelin's?"

"No hard feelings." I gave her an understanding smile to show I meant it.

I couldn't stand Brenda biting her lip in dejection over Brian, so I went back outside. Even though it wasn't dark yet, the bars had already turned on their outside lights to signal they were open for business. Looking down the street, I could see my green bulb over La Vida, the twin amber globes flanking the thick wooden door of the Minibar, the cold blue glint of the Glu-Glu's sign, and the red haze from the Tiki; all in a row, like a string of Christmas lights. Music pealed out of each doorway and window like a summertime carol.

Yes, it *was* summer in Tossa! Time for smiles, suntans, dancing, getting drunk, balling. Time for all those things that really didn't matter, but made you happy. I chose the Minibar for my first summer drink because Mick Jagger's uncomplicated cock rock coming from inside seemed to best understand what I was feeling.

I had a beer and came back outside. Pete was coming up the street toward me.

"'ow's it goin'?"

"Fine, Pete . . . so fine."

The expression on his face showed he knew how high I was soaring. "Give it plenty, babe!" he yelled audaciously, tipping his floppy black corduroy cap.

It was all together now. It was summer like always. More family arriving each day. The lemon trees of the Hostalet in full bloom. Max trotting the streets, as fat and elegant as ever. All of Tossa's venerable summer institutions were in fine form. Even the Duchess had showed up last night. The old girl in that same chair in La Vida by the coffee machine from ten till closing was the one thing you could count on in Tossa every summer. The Duchess'd sip Soberanos and pass on messages in the most proper English possible, pronouncing all the syllables and aitches like the Grand English Dame she was.

I bounced along the street happy as a kid on the last day of school. I felt invincible, kind of like in those old movies where the hero cries with outstretched arms to the skyline of the teeming city, "This is my town!"

Up the block at the Gerona crossroads, I could see a policeman talking to some tall dude in a jungle camouflage jumpsuit. A large leather bag hung from his shoulder, and his pants were tucked inside his boots paratrooper style. He towered over the cop so much he appeared intimidating even to me way down the block. It was too dark to see clearly who it was, but with that long curly hair, so wild and savage in the fluorescent light, there could be no mistake.

"Bernardo!" I shouted.

He squinted in the direction of his name.

"Eh? Paul? Poppa Paul! How are you!"

It was Bernie. There was no mistaking the coarse German accent. He pulled me off the ground and crushed me in a clumsy hug. The policeman was happy at the chance to slip away unnoticed.

"Jesus! When'd you get here!"

"I come today," he boasted.

I stepped back so I could take all of Bernardo in.

"And where'd you get that freak outfit?" I was half laughing, half shaking my head with wonderment.

Bernardo laughed in agreement, gobbling up the flattery. He was so pretentiously beautiful in that ridiculous jungle suit, standing there with his hands on his hips and his legs in wide-spread defiance, wearing that four-inch belt with the lovers fucking in the lotus position on the buckle. When people first meet Bernie, they're turned off by his act. They don't realize that's really Bernardo. And after they do get to know him, they love it. He gets away with it precisely because he's that real.

"Poppa Paul, I am happy you are still here." The metal bracelets on his wrists and the beads and amulets hanging from his neck all jangled as he caught me up in another mashing hug. *"Ach!* What will I do when you are gone? Who will take care of Bernardo . . . who will be my Poppa in Tossa?

"It's good you are still here," he added tenderly, letting me go.

"Don't worry, Bernie, I'll be here long after you're gone."

"Can there be a summer in Tossa with no Bernardo!" he roared at the street without a trace of embarrassment.

"Come to La Vida for a drink," I pleaded.

"Ja . . . but later. Paul, there is no parties yet?" He asked the question like it was a matter of life and death. "This year I wish to make a great party for my birthday."

"When's that?"

"You do not remember?" He was sincerely hurt at the very idea anyone could forget. "The fifth of August."

"Bernie," my head was shaking again while I was laughing, "you're too much . . . that's not for two months yet."

"We must have a great party this year. The last year I spend my birthday in jail."

He was so serious about it, but I still couldn't stop laughing. "Who asked you to get so drunk?"

"*Ach!* You know why . . . I love her too much. I go all over Europe for her. I find she, I kill she. You remember."

I finally managed to get my laughing under control.

"She would have nothing to do with me," he went on. "That is why I drink so much." He tapped himself on the chest.

Bernardo with all his frenetic energy making things happen. Bernie the Bedouin, roaming from bar to bar in giant strides with his latest fox pulled along behind him, barely hanging on for her life. Bernie'd have a quick peek at the action, maybe one drink, and then he'd be off again looking for something that nobody had ever been able to figure out just yet. Not even Bernie! Perhaps the confusion came from his mixed blood. With that fierce Italian passion he got from his mother, he thought nothing of waking up the whole street at four in the morning while he begged Pamela to come downstairs and ball him for the simple reason he loved her. And the Prussian feistiness he inherited from his father was always getting him embroiled in fights for the vaguest reasons.

"Paul, Pamela . . . she is back this year, no?" he asked with almost life-or-death urgency.

"No. Pete said she got married last winter."

"It is true." He gulped with a sinking feeling. "I did not think she would marry without me."

"Bernie, what about all the others . . . the new ones in town already. All waiting for us," I said to try and make him forget Pamela like you would distract a baby from a lost toy.

"You are right." He tossed his head back expansively. "Poppa Paul is all the time right. You take care of me like a good father. Ah, Paul, you are good . . . so old and serious with me. We must have a great party on my birthday this year."

"Yes, Bernie," I sighed. He was exquisitely hopeless.

An unlikely somberness suddenly came over him. "I was wild for Pamela . . . the beautiful blonde hair . . . Paul . . . Paul, she was like the sun. I love her so much. Did I tell you how I chase her over all Europe? I follow her, Paul . . . to Athens . . . Belgrade . . . I catch her in Istanbul Station. I take her suitcase to stop her from the train. She tell the policeman I steal it. She wants to put me in jail—"

"I know. Pete told me . . ."

"*Ach.* She was angry . . . that beautiful face so mad with me. It makes her very sexy and I want to fuck her much more . . . I think I want to fuck her on the platform . . . there. That stupid policeman! He say I steal the suitcase. 'No,' I tell him. 'We are lovers and we fight!' I say I know all the things inside the suitcase if she will open it after. Pamela is so mad. She goes to the train." His voice dropped a rueful octave. "She was too pretty, Paul. I love her so much. I would forget my girlfriend in Munich of all these years." He threw his head back, the serious look fading. "*Ach,* no more." He was back to his normal carefree self. "Who is in Tossa? Terry and Pete. They are here?"

I nodded.

"And Big Ben."

"Everyone."

"We must have a good party. This will be a fuckin' summer, eh, Poppa Paul?" He put his arm around me. "You and me. We fuck all them!" he boasted with another arrogant roar. "Ha, ha. I go now to meet someone. A German girl I meet on the bus today. Wait! You see her, she is beautiful."

I started to say something, but he was already ambling away, eating up the street in voracious strides.

He turned to yell, "I come with her to La Vida. I think she will fuck me this night."

Days, of course, meant the beach. "A plethora of palatable pulchritude," would've been W. C. Fields' words. By mid-July the family numbered more than a hundred, spread out over the sand like a village within a village, complete with its own industries of stringing beads and making leather bracelets. We sat close to the beach bar but it was a mystery why, because any time someone wanted a beer they went into town for the bigger, cheaper bottles.

There was always a game of whist or crazy eights going (loser went for the next bottle of beer), and Phil and Horace could be found tossing the frisbee. The talk leaned toward trivia: football, work, who was new in town, who got too drunk last night—the kind of raps nobody remembered an hour later. After a long stretch of these sunny days you found yourself waking up in the morning praying for rain, just for the sake of the change. And yet no matter how stale the routine got, you still came to the beach every day, because there's a special serenity in being among friends under a clear blue sky with the town and hills behind you alive with summer.

A birthday, someone leaving, anything different was reason enough for a beach party. Terry would wade through the sprawled bodies, pushing his green rain hat in your face, babbling like a carnival barker. "All right yeh blokes, give us twenty-five pesetas now for the bubbly. Come on . . . come on. I've got a right thirst on!"

When Horace's van came back with the crates of champagne, the family sprang to life. We'd be up off the sand grabbing for the cold bottles. POP! POP! POP! An artillery barrage of exploding corks hailed down as the champagne spewed all over, drenching everyone. We would dance . . . and dance . . . and dance to someone's guitar or cassettes, raising our bottles to the white-hot sky with crazy war whoops.

At the first party of the summer Brian was dancing with Dominique. He'd been hustling her since that first night she'd waited on him in the Bivak. Dominique came to a stop in the middle of the song. "I forget I am to give propaganda today."

"I'll help you," Brian said, following her away from the pack.

"I never like this," she sighed, picking up the stack of advertising cards.

"Come on, it won't take long if we both do it." He held his hand out for some cards.

I watched them move through the crowd. Dominique with her brown hair boyishly cropped at the top of her long neck glided like a swan through the clusters of afternoon sunbathers. The two pieces of her green pastel bikini, so dull on her pale skin at the start of summer, were now the perfect trimmings for her suntanned body.

I was trying to score either of two Irish sisters on holiday who had wandered into our party. Behind them stood Brenda talking with Bernardo, but her eyes followed Brian and Dominique.

Maybe Bernardo was trying to take Brenda's mind off Brian, or maybe he was just feeling devilish. I don't know which, but that wild, brawling look when he'd had too much to drink came over his face.

"Brenda, I am very hot. *Ja!* We need a bath!" he yelled so everyone could hear him.

All of a sudden Bernardo scooped Brenda up in his arms and was heading for the water. She kicked the air uselessly, threatening, "Bernie . . . don't yer dare, Bernie. No! Bernardo! I just done me 'air!" But Bernie was too drunk to care. He staggered and stumbled over people and blankets, but stayed on course, making for the sea. At the high tide mark where the sand sloped down, Bernie missed the change in level. His step off the rise was an almost toppling lurch that he turned miraculously at the last possible moment into a half-spin. Everyone applauded the pirouette. Facing us, Bernie hoisted Brenda in triumphant answer to our cheers, and then he turned back to the water.

Brenda gave up the struggle. She went limp in Bernie's arms, resigned to her fate. That was when Bernie stepped in some kid's sand bucket and they both crashed headlong, with Brenda reaching out to break her fall. Bernie lay there as if dead, face down in the sand. He didn't so much as twitch. He'd completely bombed out again in classic Bernardo fashion.

"Ow . . . me arm . . . me bleedin' arm," Brenda wailed, sitting up. "I think I broke me bleedin' wrist." She threw sand with her good hand at the unsympathetic, still body. "Fuck yeh, Bernardo!"

"Quick, doctor! Anesthetic fer the little gearbox!" Terry screamed, running up to offer his champagne bottle.

Everyone was laughing but Brenda. She turned away from the champagne with a grimace of pain. "Shit! 'ow the bleedin' 'ell am I gonna work with a broken wrist?"

Everyone became hushed when they realized she was really hurt. I started over to help Brenda, sadly leaving my splendid Irish quail fair game for anyone. When I arrived at the high tide crest, I could see why I couldn't find Phil or Pete to team up with me on the two sisters. Both were passed out at the water's edge as "dead" as Bernardo. I yelled for someone to pick them up. They could've drowned there when the tide came in.

Brenda cradled her wrist in her other arm as we started for the doctor. We passed Terry and some of the others stacking Phil and Pete and Bernardo and all the other party debris in the back of Horace's van. Three dead and one walking wounded. A good party, I decided. And maybe an Irish fox that night too, I hoped, as I remembered to yell an invitation to the sisters to come by La Vida later for a drink.

Brenda came out of the doctor's office with her wrist in a sling. That it was only a sprain was a kind of relieved joy. I walked her up the hill to her place. At the door she said, "Thanks, Paul. Yeh know it should've bin Brian doin' this." I watched her biting her lip again. "I guess we really are finished now . . . sort of before it started," she went on gamely.

"Hey, Brenda, you know the rules of summer. You been here long enough." I know I sounded callous, but it was the only way I could think of to stop her feeling sorry for herself.

She nodded sullenly. "I just always fancy yeh yanks. That's me trouble." Her dark eyes gave a long look, the kind I had seen a lot the previous summer. "Paul, I can't fancy bein' alone tonight."

"I'll see you at Sivas after I close," I said, thinking I'd have to be careful about that sprain. But down deep I really knew she wouldn't want to do anything but be held and comforted.

The bars closed earlier than the discotheques, so everyone always ended up at Sivas. It wasn't that Sivas was so great that made the family go there, it was that we didn't have to pay at the door. And besides, Pete was the best disc jockey in town. He was always tuned in to the crowd, keeping things swinging, mixing the strobes and colored lights, and drawing the dancers and those of us on the sidelines playing "invisible guitars" to a frenzy with numbers like *Jumping Jack Flash* or *Are You Ready*. And then when you thought there wasn't another boojie-woojie beat left in your wrung-out, sweating body, *Born to Be Wild* or some other rocking number came on to bring new heights of screaming "yah-yah's" and upraised arms throttling the red air.

I was standing at the bar in Sivas with Ben that first night he met Randi. The previous night with that seventeen-year-old Norwegian beaver had been enough for me, but Sivas was so packed it didn't seem worth the jostling in the crowd just to avoid her. When Randi saw me, she came over. I introduced her to Ben, ready to split at the first opportunity.

There was nothing special about their first meeting. Maybe I only remember it because of the effect Randi had on Ben. But even that would not have been important, except now I see Ben was a harbinger, not only of all these events, but more so of what was to happen to me.

Randi'd come into La Vida the night before and stayed till I closed. I was only going to walk with her as far as Sivas, but instead we ended up back at her pension balling on the bathroom floor because her boyfriend was asleep in their room down the hall. That little Norwegian fox was on one really weird trip. The first time, she sat on the can while I balled her and tried to shit at the precise moment she came.

The second ball was better with that lush, plump ass riding on top. She had the natural rhythm of a rocking chair in those big hips. Her moans took off to agonizing levels in the bathroom; they seemed loud enough to wake the whole town. Afterward we were stretched out on the cold tile in each other's arms like exhausted milers. I kept asking myself, what was I doing there? The first ball on the john was kinky fun, but I wasn't really getting it off—not in my head. Now that we were finished, we lay on the floor saying nothing, just letting out an occasional restless sigh. I could find nothing better to do than watch the upsweep of the underside of the toilet bowl.

"I have a daughter. She must be about your age," I murmured at one point, frustrated by the silence.

"That's nice," she answered. Her palm stirred and came to rest on my thigh, making a headline flash across the white porcelain of the toilet bowl.

AMERICAN BAR OWNER FOUND WITH

NYMPHET IN W.C. AT 4 AM

I lay my hand like a roadblock in front of her creeping fingers. She went to nibbling my ear. *The little minx was working up to full speed again! So soon!*

AMERICAN BAR OWNER FOUND

MYSTERIOUSLY DEAD IN W.C.

WITH HIS DAUGHTER(?)

I stood up to dress. She wouldn't give me my shirt. She kept pulling it up between her legs and then caping me over the head with it. I tried to put her off by saying it was too close to morning. That made the little bitch taunt me even more, offering me my shirt and then pulling it back with a childish giggle. I wanted to haul off and smack her like you would a brat. I was putting on my pants after giving up on my shirt when she ran out of the bathroom and locked me in. She threatened to leave me for the landlady in the morning if I wouldn't ball her again. She wouldn't hear of anything else. Jesus Christ! It was insane! I tried to make it with her, just to get the hell out of there, but I couldn't. There was nothing left inside me at that point . . . nothing but anger and shame.

With Big Ben and Randi it was different. They were together incessantly for two days before it dawned on anyone it was for real. They were content to be by themselves at the far end of the beach near the castle. The boyfriend left Tossa and Randi moved in with Ben. It was the fairy tale of the summer: the ugly frog changed into a prince by the fair princess. The two of them would sit all night at Max's corner of the bar holding hands. The glitter in Ben's eyes had enough electricity to light Tossa for the whole summer. Even his Fu Manchu moustache lost its brooding evil. Randi glowed too, brighter than her lobster-red fair skin would after a day on the beach. Brenda called them "cute." "Sweet as a filbert," Phil would say each time he saw them at the other end of the bar. The puppy love even got to me. I was buying them rounds and afterwards the two of them would weave drunkenly out the door, only to come back a few minutes later with a gift of lemons stolen off the trees at the Hostalet.

Sure, Randi was young enough to be Ben's daughter too, but in this case it was different. She was good for him. For the first time since I'd known Ben, he was off the pills. He was alive! Christ, he was even dancing at Sivas, something I'd never seen him do before. He'd jump around in clumsy paroxysms, flailing those immense paws and pleading with Pete to play *Bitch* just one more time.

A summer storm had knocked out all the electricity in town. In the candlelight and without the jarring rock and roll, Tossa was a beautiful throwback to the turn of the century. The lack of a musical background created a sense of shyness in the bar. Everyone was put off their stride, less sure of themselves, as if the silence left them naked and exposed.

The rain had kept things slow, so there had been time to play chess with Raoul. An early stupid move in the game had cost me my queen. Checkmate was inevitable for the second time because I wasn't concentrating. I'd been thinking about Christiane. Her vacation was over and she'd gone back to Paris that morning. It had never mattered before when a fox left, even a Parisian like Chris, who possessed all those little nuances of the French I love so much: the way they eat so meticulously, hold their cigarettes so delicately, or wear the gaudy jewelry that looks so perfect on them, but so tacky on everyone else.

I'd lived with a lot of other foxes during the summers who were in their early twenties like Chris, but for the first time the years intruded on the easiness of a holiday affair. After the first few days, the nights became long and restless. There was nothing else to share but the balling. I could only listen to her talk about the Beatles or Viet Nam or hashish, saying nothing. She didn't know who James Dean was or what the Korean War was all about or anything else out of the prophylactic fifties when I'd been her age. Maybe it was like this for me with all the others, too, *but this time I noticed!* There would be these sudden flashes of loneliness I had not felt since I watched them lower my father's plain pine box into the grave.

When Brian came in the bar, I toppled my king to the board. "Enough! Enough!" I pleaded, conceding the game to Raoul. "You've won both games tonight. I must be getting lazy."

"It is because it is too easy for you, Pablo. You enjoy the summer while I chase *grupúsculos* in the hills."

"Yeah, it's softer than the Queen's ass working every night till dawn," I said indifferently, letting out a yawn.

"Perhaps it is the work in bed after you close that tires you. Maybe you had better *retire* from it." He laughed at his pun with much relish.

The taunt struck too close to home to be funny. Raoul sensed that from my look. Tactfully he turned his attention to Brian. "*Señor* McCabe, for one who was leaving Tossa, you have stayed a long time. You wish to play that game of chess? Tonight I could defeat God!"

"Not tonight then," Brian said with a friendly grin. "You've scared me off."

Brian reached for an old *Newsweek* on the window sill. The cover had a photo of an American soldier in Viet Nam.

"Were you in the war?" Raoul asked, catching sight of the picture as Brian dropped the magazine back on the sill.

"Yes."

"Combat?"

"For a time," Brian answered, after a moment's hesitation.

"My family was always military," Raoul said. "That is why I am *Guardia.* My father was an officer with *El Caudillo* from the beginning at Morocco," he added with great pride.

"I have read some books on the Civil War."

"Which books?" Raoul questioned.

"You might not like it," Brian said with a tease.

Raoul smiled confidently. "Pablo will tell you it is all right to speak your heart to me. I am a realist about our history."

I nodded when Brian looked to me. *"For Whom the Bell Tolls. Days of Hope* by Malraux," he said.

"Good books," Raoul confirmed. "I read Hemingway when I was a student in your country, and Malraux too. They speak the truth of war, but their politics are not right for Spain."

"And your soldiers and guns are?"

"My young friend, I will admit I was for Franco in the beginning because of my family, but now I am old and no longer believe in the purity of causes—Nationalist or Republican. But Franco is still best for our country. You have read of all the killing and hatred of our war," Raoul said rhetorically. "This is not America. We do not have your space or your rich earth to grow things, or even the hungry ambitions of immigrant fathers who are driven to make a prosperous life. Still, lacking these talents and the burden of a terrible war of Spaniards killing Spaniards, Franco brought Spain comfort and honor. He brought us all this you now enjoy. It is not so bad when you think of the start. I ask you how it would be if the Republic was victorious? A government made up of priest-murdering Basques and communists and anarchists from *Cataluña.* Between them and all the others, they would've pulled Spain to pieces. They could only have failed because they were so many parties. And who would have Spain then?"

He paused a moment, biting his lip. "Hitler. Or the Vichy of France," he went on with obvious disgust. "Think of it that way, *Señor* McCabe. Do not judge our government by yours. Think only of what Franco has made of Spain and where we would be without him."

Brian could see Raoul was sincere in this belief. He was not some fascist lackey spouting the party line.

"I never thought of it that way," Brian said. "Perhaps the good and bad of your cause was not that clear. But the war was bad."

"Yes, and then . . ." Raoul gazed thoughtfully at the *Newsweek* cover. "War is fascinating to the Spanish because death is so abundant, so accessible. In war, we can study death, dissect it into all its pieces, see it from every possibility."

"That's why bullfighting is so important to you, isn't it?" Brian said.

"Exactly! You Americans are so different. You try to ignore death. What is interesting is how you analyze sex, like we do death . . . and," Raoul smiled as the idea came to him, "we treat sex like you do death. We keep it in the closet."

"I've got the feeling you understand killing and war," Brian said.

"When it is necessary, *amigo,*" Raoul answered. "It is part of one's duty to one's country and family honor."

"You were in combat too?" Brian asked like an understanding brother.

"Yes."

"The Spanish Civil War?" Brian wondered uncertainly, I guess, trying to count the years. I'd never thought to ask Raoul about any of this before.

"I was too young," Raoul said, brushing him off curtly. He went to the open doorway, looking thoughtfully into the dark street. "Without electricity Tossa is even better, I think. I would have enjoyed life in the nineteenth century. Everything was more exact, much clearer. Well . . ." His hand reached out to test for rain. "I think the storm is finished. If no one wishes to play chess, *buenas noches.*"

We watched him pass each of the bar windows until he was out of sight.

"I guess he's too ashamed of the killing to talk about it. I know how he feels," Brian said.

The last time I saw Randi she was with Ben in their special corner of the bar. They were in street clothes and hadn't been to the beach, even though it was a beautiful day. They sat without ordering, without even a word between them.

"Anything before I go upstairs to change?" I asked.

"Nothing now," Ben said, with a listlessness I hadn't seen in him since meeting Randi.

"If you're out of money, Ben, you know your credit's good with me."

"It's not that." His eyes were red cat's-eye marbles. "We're just drunk out, that's all."

"You do look like hell," I agreed, trying to sound humorous, but it didn't make the slightest dent.

"Randi's leaving. We were up all night to have all the time together we could."

"I do not leave now," Randi wrenched the words out. "The plane is gone without me."

"She was supposed to catch the morning bus," Ben explained. "But we couldn't do it, so we decided to get a taxi, and then we figured we could wait awhile longer, and then . . ." His face screwed tight as he sat up straight. "We've been drinking all afternoon and everything's too late now," he muttered sadly.

"I see," was all I could think to say.

Ben didn't seem to hear me. He went on, oblivious to everything else. "We couldn't get up from the table. We just sat there and kept drinking and now . . ."

"Why go back, Randi? Summer's only half gone. There'll be plenty of rides north at the end of summer." I didn't really care if the little blonde muff stayed or not, except for Ben's sake.

"I must return home. I am serious for school. I must study before school commences. Every year I am not serious. Now, I must make my examinations. I am happy with Ben because I was to be serious in school. If I do not go home then I feel bad because it was all not true what we have."

"Can you dig that?" Ben said flatly and without hope.

"I could not leave Ben, and now I have missed my charter and I have no money."

"Don't worry. I'll get you a plane ticket," Ben reassured her. Somehow he sounded heroic, when he should've sounded ridiculous. I shouldn't have felt sorry for someone like Ben who'd been around too long to get hung up on pussy young enough to be his daughter. Why couldn't he have made it a one night frolic like I had?

"You do not have that much money!" Randi cried. "Come. I go to use the telephone to my home."

Ben wouldn't move. She pulled at his sleeve.

"One more drink and then we go," he begged, looking at me rather than her.

"No. This is no good. We go to the telephone office. Please, Ben."

Ben lingered and finally he let her pull him off the bar stool. They shuffled outside like prisoners going to their execution.

Brian was there the next afternoon when Ben came in the bar. "Well, she's gone," Ben said with a forced wave of his hand, trying to be casual. "God, that was crazy," he mused after sitting down next to Brian and trying so hard to seem detached.

"Ben, you know she's the greatest thing that happened to you here," Brian said, draping his arm over his shoulder. "For once in your life, you weren't watching the beach. Come on. You helped her pull it all together, too."

Ben seemed to ignore Brian's remark. "A beer, Paul. Summer's so unreal here. She's probably different at home with her family. I bet she'll go back to that boyfriend." He started to reach for his beer and then didn't take it. "Aw, fuck. I'd feel like an ass running around school with her. I'm twice her age, God damn it. I shouldn't even be here myself. You know, on the way back from the airport I felt so crazy and strange. I'm driving along and suddenly this damed awful loneliness is in me, like when you wake up by yourself in the middle of the night. I couldn't get away from it. I tried to think about the sea, about drinking, about Randi. . . .

"Nothing helped. I felt old, can you dig it? And then I realized that the loneliness I was feeling was my home, my wife and kids . . . all gone. Don't you see, that's what Randi was filling up for me. To tell you the truth, we didn't even ball much after the first few days. For me summer's over. I'm going home."

"Hey, come on, man!" I pleaded. "What is there for you back there? You'll be that same old suburban buffalo again. It doesn't change, Ben."

"That's right, but at least that's something. There's nothing here. Don't you see that?"

"Ben, two hours after you're back you'll wish you were here."

"I know," he sighed softly.

"Brian, talk to the damn fool!" I was almost yelling. Me, who always told myself to stay on my side of the bar and just listen, nothing more?

"No more summers for me, Paul," Ben said. "It took Randi to make me realize that. You know why she liked me so much. I was the first guy she'd been with who didn't care about her fucking all the others. Yeah, Paul, she even told me about that time in the john."

I poured myself a drink, for I had this sudden urge to appear busy.

"What can I tell you," Ben went on, "except what I told her. I just didn't want her to leave. Just like some dumb little schoolboy I kept repeating that to her right up to the end."

"That's the most beautiful thing you can tell anyone, Ben. I envy you that," Brian said.

We all were quiet for a while. Ben broke the silence.

"I'm going to call my wife. I've got to make myself do it. I'm going back home whether she'll have me or not. But first another round of beers and shots of tequila, too!"

"Not for me. I've got to work tonight," I said.

Ben looked to Brian to see if he was being totally deserted. Then they both looked at me like I was the traitor. I poured the three shots. "Only one for me. I mean it," I said, and we knocked the shots back.

Ben never got to the phone that night. He and Brian sat there drinking the tequila and beer chasers right through dinner, through the Minibar, the Tiki and all the other bars on the street before heading for the Llibertat. Bernardo was with them for a while, but he faded fast. Bernie never could handle the cactus juice. They finally ended up at Sivas with faithful Brian, still at Ben's side, passed out along the wall while the Big Bear kept hopping around the dance floor to *Bitch* each time he could talk Pete into playing it one more time.

The next day everyone was on the beach early. It was too damn hot to be anywhere else or do anything but lie in your sweat, soaking up the heat from the sand.

Ben staggered up to the group around two, holding a big bottle of beer by the neck. He was in worse shape than the previous night, more stumbling, lousy drunk, and with the unmistakable glaze of uppers back in his eyes.

"'ey Ben, where yeh bin? Sit 'ere with us," Pete said with extra camaraderie before he went back to his hand of crazy eights.

Ben took a long draught of the half-filled bottle and plopped down clumsily with his back to the card game. "I made the call this morning. I'm going back. Sylvia and I are gonna try again." It's the only time I ever remember him referring to his wife by name. "She is too good." He offered the bottle to the rest of us, but no one wanted any. He gulped down another long swig of beer. "Oh God, Brian, what am I gonna do back there! I don't belong anywhere."

"Last card!" Pete yelled, plunking a card down on the deck. "Let's make it spades, mates." He kept a poker face as he looked around the game while the other players tried to decide if he was lying.

Suddenly Ben's head was rolling. He had that unsteady look I'd seen in La Vida too many times. He toppled backwards right into the center of the card game.

"'ere now . . . come on, Ben," Pete growled. "Don't bugger up this 'and." But Pete's pleas were useless. The huge bear was face up in the sun with the beer spilling out of the bottle, forming a dark brown stain on the sand. "On yer bike . . . Ben! 'ey Ben!" Pete's voice lowered. "Fuckin' 'e's two and eight, 'e is . . . the big bloke." He poked Ben gently with the lone card in his hand. "Well, let's move the game . . . don't want to stop it. I've got me a winnah this round."

They swept up the cards from beneath Ben's wreckage and moved to the other side of the family.

Brian looked at his friend. "Nothing we can do but let him sleep it off. Looks like he started early today."

"I don't think 'e's ever stopped from yesterday," someone bantered.

"Who's going in the water?" someone else yelled. A bunch of us started for the shoreline, leaving Ben all by himself, away from the mainstream of the family.

The sea was warm and quiet as death. We waded slowly into the water without the usual crashing dives or dunkings because it was too damned hot for horseplay. It was even too hot for the little white paddle boats to be shuffling around the cove. Everyone was content to be left alone to float peacefully on the tepid calm that was broken only once by the slow strokes of a passing swimmer.

Brian, Dominique, and I came out of the water at the same time. Maybe a half hour later, at most. Near our towels Ben was still face up in the sun. When we came close I could see the yellowish bile at the corners of his mouth, drying in his moustache. The level of the beer had stabilized in the bottle, no longer dripping onto the sand. Dominique started cleaning up Ben's face with her towel.

"Jesus!" I said. "I've never seen him this far gone." I tried to shake him awake. "Ben, come on, Ben."

"Ben. Ben." Brian shook him too. "Someone get some water. That'll wake him up . . . Ben."

Brian was staring at the pasty face like he'd noticed something he hadn't seen before. "Ben!" he shrieked, completely shattering the afternoon calm. Everyone in the family turned. It was the loudest sound we'd ever heard from Brian.

"Ben, God damn you!" Brian cried even louder than before, shaking Ben's flabby mass as punishment. He put his ear to Ben's chest. I could see the pain of scratching needles in Brian's blue eyes.

Brian pulled back from the hairy chest, sweaty sand stuck on his ear.

"He's dead," he whispered, sucking at the hot air for breath.

"Choke to fuckin' death on yer own vomit while yer bloody well starin' at 'eaven. What a fuckin' miserable way to die," Pete said as he stirred his coffee.

Brian was still in his bathing suit. He had just come back from taking the *Guardia* over to Ben's apartment to find an address to notify the family. "It don't make one bit of difference how it happens," he said. "Like this or turned to tapioca by a mortar shell while you're jerking off in your tent."

Pete slid off his bar stool. "Well, mates, must be off, but I can't say's I'm in the mood to chat up birds or make music. I reckon it won't be such a good night."

After I'd finished washing the cups and glasses from the afternoon business, I found Brian staring out the window at his motorcycle. It had stood unused against the wall all summer. "We ought to write Randi," he said. "You know her address?"

"Someone'll have it."

"It'd really be bad if she never knew. Dumb fucking Ben. He had to go back to watching the beach, didn't he." His breath eased out in a sigh of disgust. "I should've died instead of him, Paul."

"What kind of fucking talk is that!"

"Ben had a reason not to die. I didn't."

"That's a crock of shit and you know it." Up till now I thought I'd stayed pretty much together over Ben's death, but there I was fumbling for words.

"Paul, I envy how you can just kind of live like this, rolling along, grabbing a piece when you can and hitting a new place every winter. But I don't work like that. I'm like Ben. I've got to have reasons."

"Brian . . ."

He cut me off. "The irony is you may be the one better off, Paul, because sometimes I get scared that maybe you're right—maybe the world is one big gigantic fuck!"

How could I tell him it was only the years that made it that way for me and not for him? He still had the capital of his youth to spend on trying to stop the inevitable. I was really glad the layers of disappointment hadn't started piling up on him yet like they had on me . . . and Ben, who couldn't carry it anymore. Anything's better than ending up like Ben, washed up on the beach like one of those ugly Portuguese men-of-war all tangled up in seaweed. But I couldn't bring myself to say any of this to Brian. After all, it was summer in Tossa, I told myself, looking around, and that made the serious words so unreal.

We had passed the fulcrum point of the summer and were coasting downhill toward the end. The hot day of Ben's death had been a signal, for the summer abruptly turned on its heels and attacked us with a spell of sticky weather. The heat was like thick gauze covering everything. It created an inertia that made Tossa seem to move in slow motion. The wells, always overburdened by the tourist invasion, had dried up earlier than usual, now pumping only salt water. Finally one night the heat, building up layer by layer over the days, wouldn't even dissipate after the sun went down.

It had been pretty slow in the bar, so I sent Bonnie home early. I sat, waiting to close, with only one last couple at the bar. They were drinking Cuba libres, huddled so ludicrously close in the heat I couldn't bear to watch them any longer. I went back to the storeroom to get the carafe of fresh water to fill the ice trays for the next day.

Brian was at the bar when I returned. "I didn't expect to see you again tonight. Where's Dominique?" I asked.

"She's gone to bed. We were both too bitchy with each other from this damn heat." He looked down at the rings of perspiration on his T-shirt. "How a moonlight swim would make it tonight . . . anything different."

"You know the police won't let you," I said. A rumble of thunder growled overhead. "It sounded like it came from behind the hills. That's a good sign. Maybe it'll break tonight."

"A nightcap?" I asked.

"How about *Sangria?*"

"Come on! That's too much trouble to make."

"You asked," he taunted. "Ok, a beer then. But ice cold."

The couple got up to leave. I locked the door after them and turned off the green light over the door.

"Why you so hard on Dominique lately?" I asked.

"It's not her fault. I'm just in a funk these days."

"Because of Big Ben?"

"That's some of it, but not really the whole thing. Paul, you get the feeling his death's had absolutely no effect here? Things just seem to go on for everyone, as if Ben never happened. He wasn't even a ripple in the pond."

"People don't come to Tossa to remember."

He brooded for a moment on my words. "The level of thought here wouldn't tax the village idiot," he finally said. He could see I wasn't following him. "You'd think our lives would revolve around something besides drinking and fucking," he went on. "It's really banal on those beach blankets. Thank God this heat wave came along or there'd be nothing new to talk about."

"Brian, no one thinks in paradise."

"I don't expect everyone to read books and then have a debate, but you'd think the conversation would, at some point, take on substance . . . about something that requires 'thought.'"

"Like what?"

"Come on!" He moved away from the bar in disgust, as if he wanted to drop the whole thing. "You know what I mean."

I wouldn't let it go there. I said, "That's all a crock of shit, so why do you care?" I had almost automatically thrown out the words, mostly in reaction to my own irritation with the heat and boredom of the late summer.

Brian must've been feeling the same things, for he wouldn't let it go now, either. "You know, Paul, outside of your peculiar brand of nihilism I never glean one new idea here. I'm surrounded by Europeans and all I get out of it is the best brand of beer to drink in each country. In Tossa we exchange customs, not cultures."

The town clock struck the three o'clock closing hour. I rechecked all the locked doors out of sheer force of habit. There were still some people strolling the streets in zombie fashion, as if motion was the only way to live with the heat.

"Do you want to close up and go to bed?" Brian asked.

"No, it's too hot to sleep." The heat didn't stop the small grin from coming over my face as I added, "It's even too hot to ball."

That got a laugh out of Brian, and for a minute we both seemed to forget the heat. Then the sober reflection that would sometimes suddenly come over his face was there. "Paul, why do you stay? How do you stand Tossa year in and year out?"

"I work so hard I guess there's no time to think about it," I said. But the joke didn't satisfy him. "Brian, you can't sit and watch the beach, like you told Ben. You can't come back year after year and just hang out. For people like you, Tossa's only some place to catch your breath. There are no answers here. Get a good tan and all the ass you can, and split when it's over like all the good tourists."

The handle and frame of the door rattled from someone's jiggling. I signalled I was closed. The two couples glumly moved away. The conversation couldn't seem to get going again after the interruption.

"Everyone will be at the Llibertat after Sivas closes. You want to go up there?" I asked after a while.

"No. No." He had clenched his fists at the very idea. "That's the place I don't want to go tonight. I'm tired of all that same shit."

His thonged sandals slapped the floor as he paced over to the open window to stare through the bars. A flash of lightning lit up the doorways of the buildings across the street. They were as empty as their darkness implied.

"Maybe I'm thinking about Big Ben after all, Paul. I'm afraid I'm going to end up like him. I'm more afraid of watching the beach than anything. That's what gets me about Dominique. She's happy like you to just float along and . . ." His words trailed off as if absorbed by the heat. Then I could hear his soft voice again. "There has to be at least one irrevocable act in your life. That's the only way you know you exist."

"If that's so, how can you stay here?"

"Tossa was to be a resting place. And some human contact again. I'd been alone for so long. And because of you too. You've been my best friend in a long time. Someone I could talk to. I wish I could give you as much. Summer here fits my life so neatly. People always passing through, just like you said, no one staying. You meet without warning on the beach or in the street, get together at the bar for a few drinks, have a dance or two at Sivas . . . and maybe bed. We both don't have to give anything here because we both already know when the ending will happen even before we start. For someone who has nothing it's the perfect place."

"Christ, you sound like a criminal on the lam."

Brian eased his tension with a grin. "No, that was how I ended up in the army. My father pulled strings to get me off a dope dealing bust if I'd enlist. At the time, it didn't make any difference to me—jail or the army. Both were the same. The war came to mean something to me for a while. And then that died too."

"How?"

"It's not worth getting into," he said with a shrug.

It had begun to rain. At first it was only a few drops drumming on the windowpane in irregular beats, and then a blitz of water. Vapors of steam rose in the glow of the street lights, unlocking the heat from the pavement.

"It's broken at last," Brian said and rushed back to the open window to listen to the storm. "I love the cleansing smell of a big rain."

"Like being reborn," I said.

The cascading downpour lit up like tinsel in the next flash of lightning. Whatever Brian muttered was drowned by the roar of the storm, but I swear it was something about "a second chance never seems to make a difference." The storm slowed to a steady shower. "I'm sorry we got into all this tonight," he said.

"What else are friends for," I said, but with that impotency when you know there's no way you can really help, except to say "I know."

"I think I'll walk in the rain for a bit. It'll cool me off," he said.

He opened the door. The roar of the storm became louder, then hushed again when he closed the door after him. I went to turn off the lights and noticed I'd forgotten to clean up after the last couple. Their glasses were as close together on the bar as their bodies had been, and the ice in the leftover Coca-Cola had melted into the depressing color of shit.

Bernardo, Pete and Brian had the bored look of late summer on their faces as they sat at the bar in La Vida drinking Pernod for a change of pace. Bernardo restlessly pawed the crossbar of his barstool. "Today is the first day of August, no?" he asked.

"Fuckin' right. I know. The rent's due and I'm skint," Pete said dejectedly.

"My birthday, it comes in five days. This year we have a great party!" Bernardo announced in his own special brand of self-centered optimism.

"It'd get things moving," Brian agreed.

"The greatest party in all of Tossa!" Bernardo roared. "You help too, eh, Poppa Paul?"

"No, Bernardo, I got to work in the bar." I knew better than to get involved in Bernardo's schemes.

But Bernie was undaunted. "You, yes Pete?" he insisted.

"Right."

"We have the party on the beach . . . after Sivas closes," Bernardo went on, his bracelets jangling as he slapped the bar for emphasis.

"Fuckin' bottles of champagne . . . and sandwiches," Pete crowed, caught up in the excitement. "I'm bloody good at makin' sandwiches. Everyone will be pissed as a newt!" He was hooked good. He forced down the last of his Pernod with a sour face and pushed the empty glass away. "Paul, give us a beer. I can't stand anymore of this frog shit!"

"You know they won't let you have a party on the beach at four in the morning," I said, but knowing it was really useless to argue. I was already beginning to feel sorry for them.

"We go outside Tossa. Perhaps the little beach near Giverola!" Bernardo suggested. He was becoming more enraptured with the plan each minute. "We go on your motorcycle tomorrow and see, yes, Brian? No words to no one. Only workers for this party. This must be a secret." He held his fingers to his lips, looking around at the three of us.

"It'd work, Paul," Brian said. The enthusiam had infected him also. I said nothing. They were all too far gone by then.

That night they were already collecting the fifty pesetas apiece for the food and champagne. It was supposed to be only for the family, but of course, with Bernardo handling it, everyone in town knew about the party inside of two days. Tourists who'd just arrived would come into La Vida with their 50 p's asking for Bernardo. Amazingly, though, it was really coming together. On the day of the party they bought three hundred bottles of champagne and carried one hundred and fifty loaves of bread in blanket slings up to Bernie's apartment. Nobody saw the three of them all day. They were too busy cranking out the sandwiches. By eight o'clock that evening they had everything in Horace's van, ready to go.

So the police couldn't break it up, the crux of the security was that nobody outside of the three of them knew the exact location of the party. One rumor had it the party was to be on a little beach accessible only by boat. Another had the party at a housing development where the night watchman had been paid off.

I hadn't heard anything about the police breaking it up, and that surprised me. They had to know about it—everyone else in Tossa did, right down to my Spanish maid who didn't even speak English.

If you were invited, you were to come to La Vida that night and check with the Duchess. Everyone would come into the bar and whisper to the Duchess, "Is it on?" She would faithfully give them the instructions. "After Sivas closes, look for Horace's van just past the crossroads on the coast road, and follow it."

La Vida was so wired with intrigue I was beginning to feel like Rick in *Casablanca*. All night long the bar was saturated with self-conscious conversation, as if a movie camera was filming us. I hadn't seen Brian all day, and outside of Duchesss' message I knew no more than anyone else. And finally I, *I* who knew better, thought it was actually going to happen. I went upstairs and put on my bathing trunks under my clothes.

Terry came into the bar just after I came back downstairs. His knotted-up face meant no good, even before he leaned across the bar to tell me. "They're in the nick. It's wasted."

"What?"

"They bin narked outside the Bounty."

"For what?"

Terry shrugged. "No one knows anythin' except Bernardo bashed a copper."

"Beautiful!" I had that sinking feeling for not having believed my instincts.

"They were standing outside the Bounty an' these coppers start beatin' up on this bloke—"

"With Bernie watching?" I said, finishing off his sentence as I was beginning to get the picture.

"Yeh know Bernardo and the coppers." Terry started into the story, but he didn't really have to because I already sensed what had happened. "Bernie tells 'em they can't just beat up anyone like that. Mind yeh, I see all this from the doorway of the Bounty . . . Bernardo just peels off his coat, and the coppers are watchin'. Bernie, calm as a cucumber, gives the cunt a thick lip."

"Oh, man, they were just laying for him!" I yelled. "They knew it all! They were onto the party all the time. They set them up!" La Vida lapsed into startled silence as everyone turned to see what I was shouting about. I was pissed off at everyone—the three of them in jail, my customers, the cops, the whole uptight town— but most of all I was pissed off at myself for believing in the party, even for one minute, when I should've known better.

"Them coppers all jump in from everywhere and start whackin' Bernardo. Brian come to 'elp and the next thing the lads are in the nick. It took a good eight of 'em to take Bernardo." Terry was beaming with pride at what, it occurred to me, was a pyrrhic victory.

"Who knows what the fuck they did when they got 'em inside the slammer," Terry wailed when the harsh reality of the situation came back to him.

"What about Pete?" I asked.

"'e's in the nick too. They got 'im over to the station from Sivas. 'e never came back out. Can yeh find out what's 'appenin' to 'em?"

The jail was in the town hall, in between the Bounty and the big church. This time the *Guardia* wasn't involved—it was the town cops—so me knowing Raoul made no difference. The town cops were mainly around in summer, but they're worse than the *Guardia* because the *Guardia,* for all their hangups, were still professional soldiers. The town cops hired for the summer were the dregs of the countryside who couldn't find any other work. At best, they were ignorant farmers. At worst, animals or punks. Incidents like drunks getting worked over or girls slapped around or people's money being ripped off while getting booked happened so often they were just accepted, like hangovers, as an occupational hazard of summer.

I knew better than try to see about the boys that night. It wouldn't do any good because nobody important would be around, but I went down to the jail just to calm down Terry. The night guard only shrugged off my questions. He knew nothing. I argued about finding out the charge, but it was useless. The conversation went round and round, getting nowhere. I could feel my trunks clinging thickly under my pants, climbing up my crotch as a cruel reminder I should've known better.

"'ow much to get me mates out?" Terry kept yelling when he wasn't cursing the confused guard. He kept getting louder and louder, as if shouting would make the guard understand English. I finally got him out of there. There was really nothing we could do until tomorrow, when I figured they'd let them all out with a small fine. It was standard procedure to make something like this into a drunk-and-disorderly bust.

In the morning Dominique came with us. The new guard on duty told me the charge was still unknown. He said we'd have to wait until noon for the mayor. Now I was worried. The mayor meant a heavy trip, not some routine, trivial fine. There was nothing to do but go to the Bar Simon and drink coffee.

The mayor wasn't there at noon either, but the guard had the bad news. I turned to Terry and Dominique. "They want ten thousand p's each for Brian and Pete and twenty-five thousand for Bernardo."

"Ten thousand! It's fuckin' two months' wages!" Terry screamed in disbelief. His mouth had gone wide enough to hold the fines in 100 p notes. "What the fuckin' 'ell for?" he thought to ask after the shock had worn off.

"*¿Cuál es el crimen?*" I asked the guard.

The guard only shook his head. "In Spain you pay and then ask why," I said to Terry and Dominique. They were the exact words Raoul had once told me.

I asked to see my friends.

The guard took me through the steel door into a small court-yard. I didn't realize the cell was the small barred window at the other side until I heard Bernardo call out to me. "Paul, Poppa Paul." I could make him out in the dark shadows of the cell when I got near the bars. Even up close it was too dark to see if Brian or Pete were inside the same cell.

"You all right? You eaten?"

"They tell us we got to get our own food." It was Brian's voice coming from the darkness behind Bernardo.

"I'll take care of it." I catalogued the chore for later.

There was this compulsion to talk quickly, as if the guard was marking off the visit on an invisible hourglass.

Bernardo pulled his face up against the bars. "Paul, you know how much they want?"

"Yes."

"The money I give you earlier, that is some to make the fine."

"Pete, you got any bread?" I asked hurriedly.

"Two 'undred pesetas. I paid me fuckin' rent yesterday," he groaned.

"I don't have much either," Brian said. "My check doesn't come for a while."

"Don't worry. We'll get you out."

"Quick, mate. It's the black 'ole of Calcutta in 'ere," Pete said, pushing up to the window.

"How's Dominique?" Brian wanted to know.

"She's outside."

"Don't let her see this," he commanded. "Tell her I'm ok."

"You guys get wasted by the fuzz?"

"Only a little. Not much, considering how Bernardo wasted a few of them," Brian said cheerfully. That thought raised all our spirits.

"Sit tight. I'll get the bread together," I said decisively, trying to hide my concern about that promise. I was already thinking how it was Saturday afternoon and the banks were closed until Tuesday for the holiday weekend. Even with Bernardo's money, we were still forty thousand short.

"Just get us out of this shit hole," Brian begged, as if he were reading my mind.

"Hey Bernardo," I said.

"Huh?" He pushed eagerly to the bars.

"Happy birthday!" I grinned. Everyone laughed. It was the best way to end the visit.

I sent Terry for the food while Dominique and I went to the beach. The day was overcast. The few of the family who'd come down to the beach in the lousy weather, including Max, were eating last night's pâté sandwiches. "Now listen everyone!" I yelled to quell all the questions being fired at once. "They want forty-five thousand p's."

"What!"

"Holy fuck!"

"Cor blimey!"

"For what?" someone finally had the sense to ask soberly.

"I don't know. They'll only tell you after you pay."

"It's false. Zhey vill put zhem free," someone yelled in a thick German accent.

"Call the embassies! Protest!" piped up from the back.

"A fuckin' bluff," was another outcry.

"Look, the boys said they want out. They said to pay the fine," I argued.

"Zhe embassies, zhey vill help." The same thickly accented voice continued, pursuing his idea.

"It'd take too long and besides, it's a holiday weekend. They'll be there until Tuesday."

"Fuckin' blackmail! They'll pocket our cash!" Phil screamed bitterly. Everyone went quiet in the face of that very real possibility.

"Maybe," I said, "but there's nothing we can do about it. They stay in jail till Tuesday unless we raise the bread by six o'clock."

"Bread?" the Dutch boy Martin asked, holding up his pâté sandwich. "How do we get them out *mit* bread?" The English workers broke up laughing at that.

"Yeh'd pay a fuckin' fortune to get out if yeh saw that fuckin' place," Terry said, near tears. "I was in that pig sty for one night last year. It's a smelly little pit with a 'ole in the floor for a crapper. I say get 'em out."

Terry had done it. No one argued back. The decision was made!

I picked it up from there. "Be here at four with whatever bread you can afford. The fine is forty-five thousand. If everyone gives at least five hundred or more, we can do it. You know you won't get it back."

"They're doin' a stretch because they wanted a party fer us. We'll 'ave the money," Phil proclaimed for everyone.

I put on a confident grin to reaffirm Phil's pledge. Somehow without any say I was the leader of this money drive, and even worse, I would be responsible if it failed. Leadership's never been my style. It was always to be avoided because in a small place as totalitarian as Tossa, a low profile was the only survival code, doubly so if you were a foreigner and owned a business.

Dominique and I left the beach. She was all determination, confidence and gritted teeth, but the task of raising forty thousand more pesetas was settling in on me. Five hundred a person is not a lot of bread in a lot of places, but for each person in the family it was a gigantic sum when you're paid just enough to cover day-to-day expenses. The only way you get back to where you came from or where you want to go next is on whatever you can save out of your wages or the small bonus at the end of the season. What made it all even worse was that with everyone not on the beach due to the lousy weather, it meant rushing around town to try and find them, and then waiting for them to get the bread from wherever they hid their savings.

I kept acting confidently not to worry Dominique as we walked into town dividing up names of who to see. I was getting depressed, flashing more and more on what the hell it really was going to be like to get forty thousand pesetas by six o'clock. Everything was closed for the long holiday weekend and I couldn't get to my bank account until Tuesday.

Dominique sensed my despondency. She gave me a reassuring squeeze on the arm. "Paul, Brian says you are a very good friend. The best. I tell him I know you different. No one is special to you, I say to him. I see how you are now. What I say is not true. You will have the money. It is difficult . . . I know." She paused before adding, "You are not the person you want us to see."

I cleared my throat, spitting phlegm onto the street. "Ok," I told her brusquely. "Get your money. I'll find Terry to help too. We meet at the Tiki at three-thirty."

When Dominique came into the Tiki at three-thirty, Brigitte

was nagging at me from behind the bar. "You never get the money. It is too much," she lectured in her toneless Prussian accent. "Monday is best. *Ja!* You call all embassies." She had the whole thing worked out like any orderly-minded German. "The American . . . the English . . . the German consulates will be with them. They will demand a release for them on Monday."

"And run them out of town!" My voice jumped. "You know if you don't pay the fine they make you leave Spain."

"There is no assurance they will be free on Monday," Dominique argued. Her voice was strained to where the grace of her French accent was gone, but she answered Brigitte without doubt. "We will have the money."

"We'll go to the beach first to see how much they have," I said to prop up Dominique's sagging spirits. She grimly nodded.

Terry came into the bar with Horace. "Well, it's finished. Juan took the bubbly back like yeh said, Paul. We got all't. They was right nice about givin' us back the cash, the 'ole four thousand."

"Only thirty-six thousand more to go." I smiled with that sinking feeling in my stomach again.

Dominique pulled a small roll out of her jean pocket. "Here is mine." It came to more than two thousand, everything she'd saved over the summer.

"Eight 'undred more 'ere." Horace handed me a bunch of crumpled up bank notes.

"Mine's over a thousand," Terry said fatefully.

"Three thousand's all I have without the bank open," I muttered, adding the emergency fund I kept hidden in the kitchen. "Let's go down to the beach."

A few more had come down to the beach to contribute after hearing the news. Damn it, it was beautiful! People who hardly knew Brian or Bernardo or Pete gave. Two German boys who'd only been in the family a few days dropped a week's living expenses into the kitty without hesitation. Three French students whom I didn't even know by name gave the train ticket money they'd been saving to get them to the French border before hitchhiking home. Now instead, they would have the hassle of thumbing a ride out of Spain.

I had a little over nineteen thousand when I left the beach, and the clock on the church tower was already pushing five o'clock.

We split up to better cover the rest of the family. I sent Dominique and Terry to canvass Bar Simon and the other afternoon hangouts. I headed for the other side of town. Combing the apartments, I bumped into Betty on the street. She ran back to her place and met me at my next stop with her five hundred. The Dutch footballers who didn't even know anyone before last Sunday's game gave almost two thousand. Roland, from the Kikus Bar, let the blue five hundred peseta note slip from his fingers. "So the thirty-five peseta special will be my dynamite potato salad for another week," he said with a good-natured shrug.

Dominique and Terry were at the Tiki with their collections when I came in. I counted the whole lot a second time just to make sure. "Oh, shit!" I groaned. "We're sixteen hundred short and it's too late to try and find someone if you're not sure where they'll be." We stared at each other with growing deflation.

The Tiki offered everything in their till, which was only six hundred. It was five to six. I suddenly had a last-chance idea. There wasn't time to go into it. I just said, "I know where there's a thousand. Take all this over to the mayor's office and stall them till I come." Miguel, who owned the Tiki, went along to interpret for Terry and Dominique.

What made me think of Nuria for the money I'll never know, except I knew the Llibertat was sure to have that much because it had been open all day. And also, I reasoned to myself, Nuria knew all three of them, especially Brian.

The Llibertat was busy as usual. People coming off the small nearby beach at the end of the day made this one of the best times for business.

Nuria gave me an annoyed look as I took her to a corner away from the crowd. I apologized for bothering her at such a busy time.

She looked impatiently over her shoulder at the Spaniard who was now alone behind the bar. In Spanish she said, "These Spanish who come here for the summer work. The government say it is necessary to hire them. All of them, they work slow, like the old women with the nets. Terrible. But mine," she pointed. I saw him move to look busy when he saw her finger aimed at him. "He is a lazy cow . . . and stupid," she lamented.

"Nuria," I had worked it all out in my mind on the way up the hill what I would say to her. "You know Brian, my friend . . ." I said in Spanish.

"The police," she said.

"Yes," I said, relieved she already knew and was saving me the precious time of a long explanation.

"You know the problem today in Barcelona?" she asked me.

I shook my head. Just then I couldn't care less whatever she was talking about.

"I have to ask you an important thing," I said.

"One moment. I watch him with the money in the *bote*. He steals whenever it is possible."

"Nuria, please listen. I have not much time. You know my friend Brian is in jail."

She nodded. "Santiago tells me. I am sorry. It is a lot of money they wish. Gerona is worse than the Andalusians. Pigs! The Andalusians are thieves, but it is their gypsy blood that steals—"

"Nuria, I am only a thousand pesetas short and they will be free. Could you let me have it? I will pay you back however you wish."

Suddenly she was very attentive. "I never see you this way," she said, forgetting about everything else for the moment. She looked at me very intensely and then said, "I cannot give you the money."

I was stunned. "You don't have it."

"It is there in the *bote*, but your friend is in jail for stupid things. Like children, all of you!" she accused. "No, I cannot give you the money. It is not right."

"Nuria, I do not want you to give it to me. Lend it to me."

"No."

"It's important."

"It's important to me I do not give you the money."

"Nuria . . ."

"In Barcelona today, people are in prison because they hold meetings. Good people like your friends. Priests, doctors, students! Lawyers! They are not revolutionaries."

"What has that got to do with Brian?"

"Brian teaches me *hypocrite*." She said the word in English. "That word is stronger in your language. I am *hypocrite* . . ." (again in English) "if I give the money for your friends when there are more important things."

"Nuria, I will give it back to you later, tonight. I will make it in the bar tonight."

"It is not that. Today they put Catalans in prison because Basques kill somebody important in San Sebastian. The police take everyone."

"I will give you more money. Anything I can do for you, you only ask. It is getting late. I was to have the money there already. Why won't you help me?" I pleaded. "I can't help your people in

Barcelona, but you can help my friends here in Tossa."

She looked over her shoulder to the bar again. I hadn't seen her in a while. She was a shade thinner, but still foxy as ever. Cruelly so now.

"Nuria, I don't understand this at all. You know Brian. He is your friend too."

"Yes, in jail is best. He is more sensitive than all of you. The jail will make one of you summer children understand what Spain is today. *Catalunya* cannot rest until we are out of this prison too. Paul, we are all in jail. You as much as me."

"Nuria, what is all this bullshit?" I blurted out angrily in English before I caught myself. She didn't seem to understand. I started to leave and then turned back to face her, saying in Spanish, "I don't know why you want my friends to be hurt. You say you care about the people who are in prison in Barcelona for what they read or write. My friends wanted to do something no worse than that—have a party for their friends. I used to think I understood you when you were a little girl and came around my bar and would sit for hours telling me how you wanted so much to be like your father, even though you were a woman in Spain."

"*Catalunya*," she corrected me.

"Catalan! Spanish! It doesn't matter. You said the only thing you wanted was to stand tall against the bad in your country. I understood that until now. Now you are the same as the bad. You want to keep people in jail for no reason."

Her lean body didn't stir as I turned to leave. I could see the Andalusian boy looking to see if Nuria was paying attention to him as he put some money into the *bote*. I thought I saw him palm a hundred peseta note, but I didn't care enough to make sure. I was already twenty minutes late at the jail. If they were still waiting, I'd try to get them released on my word. I'd pledged the bar. That would bend the mayor for sure. He'd had his eye on my place for years.

Outside, the whole town was alive with noise. The overcast day wasn't holding Tossa back. The rich Barcelonans were already arriving, gearing up for the long holiday weekend and drinking the expensive English scotch in double measures. What did it matter if their neighbors or my friends were in jail for silly reasons? What would one of them do if I suddenly begged him for a thousand pesetas? Would he give it without question? God damn it! If I'd made the bank deposit that morning for one thousand pesetas less, I wouldn't have been hating Tossa for the first time in my life.

I didn't turn the first time I heard the sound of my name. I wasn't in the mood to talk to anyone. I hoped they were calling someone else. The second time, the call of Nuria's lilt was clear. She caught up to me, pushing a neatly folded, green thousand peseta bill into my hand and said, "My father say to me, 'Catalans must be the people to pay for *Catalunya.*' It is not fair I ask strangers to pay the price."

I didn't even have a chance to say anything. She had started back up the hill before I could even come to my senses enough to yell "Thanks!" She didn't make any sign to show she'd heard me.

Was what I was doing as absurd and foolish as Nuria thought? Maybe summer in Tossa was children's games compared to this Catalonian freedom she wanted, but summer in Tossa counted for me because it was all I had. As I started walking over to the town hall I was beginning to really feel good again, because I realized this family feeling we all had in Tossa was the best thing any of us would take away from this little town you could traverse in five minutes. Everyone who had the chance had sacrificed without question. It wasn't what I'd call heroic sacrifice because heroes have a choice—and with family there is no choice.

What did Brian say that time? "This town's so small we only have each other." While I had been counting the money in the Tiki, Brigitte had said, "Fantastic. In two hours you raise a year's wages." But now, standing in the mayor's office while they counted all thoses bills once again, I was thinking it wasn't so fantastic after all. Even double that amount, somehow the family would've come through.

When they brought the three of them up from the cell downstairs, Raoul said in his officious English, "For the English boy it is the first time you are in trouble. Bernardo, your family owns an apartment so there is nothing I can do. But *Señor* McCabe, as I recall, you were in my office a few months ago for a disturbance at the Llibertat."

"Now wait a minute, Raoul. You know that was not the same . . ." I cut in. It was the only time I can remember being angry with my friend.

Raoul shot back a disagreeable look that ordered silence. "*Señor* McCabe," he continued, "usually when a tourist has two occasions with the police they are asked to leave Tossa. As a visitor you are expected to behave no matter the situation. You are the outsider here! I am not going to ask you to leave Tossa since you are a friend of my friend, Pablo, and because you have properly paid your fine. But *Señor* McCabe . . ." Raoul's receding forehead tightened with authority, "no person has ever had occasion with me three times. Do you understand? I never see visitors to Tossa three times. And you Pablo," he said sharply, "trouble for him will be trouble for you. *¿Entiendes?*"

At the time I didn't think much of Raoul's warning to me. I attributed it solely to his duty to satisfy the mayor's anti-foreign investment policy that had been building the last few years, right along with Tossa's prosperity. "The bastards loved us foreigners before they got so rich," I grumbled out loud as we stood in the steet outside the town hall, but nobody was really paying attention.

Brian pulled a paper out of his pocket, saying, "They gave us this."

"Well, at least this whole thing was official," I said while skimming the paper. "It's no rip-off into the mayor's pockets. The money goes to Gerona. This is a list of the charges: assaulting a police officer for Bernardo and for all three of you, obstructing traffic and causing a crowd to collect in the streets."

Pete laughed. "Ten thousand pesetas for blockin' their fuckin' road. Me mum never thought I'd be worth that much."

Miguel from the Tiki said, "It no is fair. I think Raoul know, but he can do nothing. That is why Brian no must leave."

"Well mates," Pete said, "I've done a stretch in better jails is all I 'ave to say on the matter. I'm off for a long bath."

On the surface that night, everything seemed back to normal for a Saturday night. Pete was at his post at Sivas. The Barcelonans were drinking their scotch and the French were in full force because it was August, replacing the Germans who take their holidays in July. Only it wasn't all the same. Something was different that night. There was a tense truce. No one hung around in the streets. They would just dash quickly from one bar to the next with a quick glance in the direction of the police station where even the cops were staying out of sight, except for the occasional one you'd see standing on the front steps grabbing a quick smoke.

Bernardo and Brian had just come out of the Bivak. They gave each other a parting wave and Brian came inside La Vida.

"Bernardo's talking up another party," he said. "This time he knows a place along the Gerona road." Brian could hardly get the words out for laughing. "We can walk there so there'll be . . . be . . . be no complications." That broke us both up completely.

"He's freak."

"Incredible."

"You heard Raoul. He meant it," I said strictly. "I've never seem him so uptight like that before, and there's not another forty thousand pesetas in this town."

Brian gave me that big easy smile of his. "Don't worry. From now on it's going to be a quiet summer. I wouldn't even yell if I saw a tidal wave coming."

"Man, you're pretty mellow, considering."

"The world's really beautiful to me tonight. Everybody comingiup with the money like that. It was the most beautiful thing that ever happened to me. I don't know how you did it, Paul. I can't even believe it was you, you of all people."

"Yeah, yeah . . ." I was trying to shrug it off. "I don't know either."

"None of us thought you'd be able to raise all the money so fast. I had given up. I was settling down for the weekend when they came to get us. You know there's no light in that cell except for a little bulb outside the cell door, and it was always so damp and cold, even during the day. I had felt so good jumping in to help Bernardo. I never did that for anyone before. We take so much from these pigs. I was just seized with the compulsion. 'They can't do that to us!' I said to myself. And where do I end up? In a stinking dark cell with the stench of the shit hole making you gag no matter how far away you are.

"And me wondering what's going to happen—people disappear in jails like that. Brian, you dumb fuck, this is a police state—DID YOU FORGET! I was scared, Paul. I was scared because there's no one who could help me. I was as alone as Max. What was I fighting for? There I was in jail with a fine so large it blew my mind because some wild man hit a cop. And because he's my friend, right or wrong, I jumped in. I never get involved, just like you, and here I am in this miserable hole. For what?

"Now I know, Paul. Everyone giving like that and knowing they'd never get it back. This whole thing's kind of silly, really trivial in a way, but what everyone did, well . . . I feel worthwhile for the first time in a long time." He looked in the direction of the street for a moment and then turned back to me. "And you, Paul, they say you did the most."

I barely heard his "thanks," because behind us in the bar was the carefree song of all the different languages of Europe. For the moment it made me forget there was a jail in Tossa, or in Barcelona for that matter, or that there was any town in the whole world where you paid a fine and then asked why.

"Hey, *amigo*," I said to Brian, "Let me buy you a drink."

By the end of September, the Spanish sun is only a subtle glow in the sky and the waves are rushing the shore with the growing fierceness of their autumn strength. We sat quietly on the beach watching our numbers grow smaller each day.

Dominique had gone back to Paris. Her airline job had finally come through. She and Brian could only fake the kiss at the bus station . . . and the promises to meet again that winter. It never changes. *The only thing as fragile as a Tossa tan is a Tossa love.*

Bernardo had a bus ticket for the next day. And Pete and Terry were asking around for rides heading north.

Brenda and Dirty Mitch came down to the beach to say goodbye to everyone. They were heading for Morocco to look for trading beads. "I used to have a whole bag of them beads . . ." Mitch mused in his W. C. Fields drawl. "But I gave them all away . . . squandered 'em like sperm." They exchanged addresses with us and we watched them disappear down the promenade, lugging their bags toward the Gerona crossroads to start the long hitch.

"We go, all of us, to Sivas this night," Bernardo said, breaking the lull. "It will be my last night with you for another year."

Business was so slow that night I closed the bar around two. Sivas wasn't crowded, either. The few tourists and workers left were spread out, making the place look embarrassingly empty. Brian was with an American named Margaret who had wandered into town that day. She said it was ok for them to be together, since they were both fire signs. I left her to explain that to Brian and went over to keep Pete company at the d.j. booth.

The mixture of red and blue lights gave the discotheque a sentimental murkiness. Some hysterical tune by James Brown bellowed at us, the few couples on the floor dancing to it like robots. They moved mechanically, showing no expression on their faces except hope that the song would be over soon.

"God," I yelled to Pete over the noise. "Summer's dying fast this year."

Pete flipped a switch on his control board and the red light on the walls broke up into flames. He faded out James Brown and

Proud Mary came on from the other turntable, extra loud to fill up the emptiness.

> *Left a good job in the city*
> *Workin' for The Man ev'ry night an' day*
> *And I never lost one minute of sleepin'*
> *Worryin' 'bout the way things might have been*
> *Big wheel keep on turnin'*
> *Proud Mary keep on burnin'*
> *Rollin', rollin', rollin', on the river.*©

The lights flickered in time to the beat of Creedence's twangy guitars, and a few more couples warily edged out onto the floor.

Suddenly the song was over and the buzzing guitar on *Satisfaction* exploded throughout the room. Mick Jagger began screaming so loud into every corner you were completely paralyzed. You were sucked into the Stones' whirlwind of noise, pulled mercilessly down into their cavern of drums and guitars. You couldn't think! You couldn't talk! You couldn't do anything . . . but dance! The flashing light would not take *no* for an answer.

Bernardo jumped down the one step to the sunken dance floor, pulling some fox into the ring behind him. In the blinking light of the strobes, his fury of twisting hips, flapping arms, and savage curls shaking in every direction was the dance of a madman. He was a phosphorescent ghost in the instant of white light, then lost in the blackness before you saw him again in the next white flash of the strobe. Bernie flowed for all of us in the entrancing flicker of an old movie.

Like always, Bernie's madness was contagious. Everyone followed the Pied Piper of Tossa onto the dance floor, pushing the end-of-summer emptiness back into the dark corners of the room. We all bounced around, surrendering ourselves recklessly to the spell of the music.

Brown Sugar came on blasting from the speakers. Still even more Stones madness! We formed one giant circle with our arms around each other's shoulders. One at a time, someone would go into the center to jam in their own special style, with the supportive circle bobbing back and forth in time to the insistent beat. You could feel it all coming together. The charge was building in the room! Horace shuffled into the center, craning his flamingo-thin body. Then Bonnie. She slapped her feet back and forth, cracking her body like a bullwhip in the opposite direction. The perspiration poured off everyone. Beads of sweat glistened like pearls in the flashing strobes. Nothing could stop us now. The unspoken oath was written on all our shining faces. We would keep going until closing time, ignoring the fatigue of the end of summer.

Free came on with *All Right Now* and Brian was in the spotlight. His hair slapped the air in time to his favorite song of the summer. Those wonderful blue eyes travelled around the circle to each of us, but he was not the same as the others in the ring before him. We were not a supportive circle for Brian, but his army looking on from the opposite riverbank, powerless to help. No matter how close we were to him, he would always be out there by himself, caught in the hurricane eye of his own loneliness. Whatever he needed was missing inside each of us. And yet in the flashing lights, I could see the blue eyes forgiving us our flaw; they only held love for us, the kind you have for family despite their faults.

The circle broke up to Joe Cocker's rasping cries of *High Time We Went*.

> *Ain't it high time we went?*
> *Ain't it high time we went?*
> *Ain't it high time we went?*
> *Ain't it high time we went?*©

And it was. Yeah! Oh, yeah!

I was screaming now as madly as anyone. Pete left the turntable to come down there with us. We were all together now in couples and three and fours, jumping around the floor like a bunch of excited little kids, changing partners so we could dance with everyone one last time.

The girls went up on our shoulders and we kept bouncing around the floor, still faithful to the beat of the music, moving from couple to couple in a miraculous final burst of energy that found its impossible strength in the music and emotion of this last night of summer.

And then the plaintive lyrics of the Stones' *Last Time* were filling up the room:

> *Well this could be the last time*
> *This could be the last time*
> *Maybe the last time*
> *I don't know*
> *Oh no, oh no!*©

And we slowed to half-time, looking around the floor at each other with a mournful smile, knowing that some of us would come back next year, and like always, some wouldn't.

La Tardor

LA TARDOR
(Autumn)

Brian came into Paul's kitchen dressed in his swim trunks with a beach towel draped over his shoulder. His tired blue eyes managed a little shine when Paul looked up from the frying eggs on the stove.

"Margaret's gone?" Paul asked.

"She took the early bus."

"I thought you'd go to the airport with her."

"It's better this way. I hate standing around listening to flight announcements with nothing to do but look at each other."

"What now?"

"I don't know." A mirthless smile surfaced on Brian's face. "I've said that for six months, haven't I?" He restlessly looked out the window to check the weather, even though he already knew it was clear and sunny. "Right now I'm too tired to think of anything but going to the beach. We were up the whole night squeezing in the last hours."

"I bet that ain't all you were squeezing."

"There's no hope for you, Paul," Brian said with a good-natured shake of his head.

"Dirty old men need love, too," Paul called as Brian went down the steps.

Once in the street, Brian decided he wanted today to be different, not just sitting around, rooted to the usual family spot. The beach was practically deserted everywhere, giving him a wide choice of locations. The small beach below the Llibertat came to mind. He hadn't been there once the entire summer. He headed up the hill to the Llibertat where the steps in front of the bar led down to the beach.

The small beach was deserted except for the longboats and a

girl in a black bikini near the cliff. She lay on her back with Max stretched out beside her.

"A new mark, eh Max," Brian chuckled to himself as he went down the steps to the beach. He was almost upon them before he realized the girl was Nuria. Her eyes remained closed until his shadow crossed her face.

"Hello," Brian said, moving out of her sunlight.

She raised her hand to shade the glare. "Hello, Brian."

It was the first time he'd seen her in the daytime, the first time dressed in anything but dark slacks and a pullover. Without makeup the tough scrutiny of the sun made her look younger, more like her nineteen years. The long working hours of summer had thinned her out to where her ribs were as visible as Max's had been in winter.

"I never see you on the beach," Brian said.

She sat up, leaning back against her palms. "I no like the beach in summer. All the times too much peoples."

"So now you come out for your tan."

Already the sun had freckled her nose, but he hadn't noticed it when he was in the Llibertat with Margaret the night before.

"Where is Margaret?" she asked.

"She left today to go back to the States."

"She was very nice."

"I liked her very much," he agreed.

"You like all the girls." Her sarcasm made him laugh. "You leave Tossa?" she asked.

"Soon. I think I'll go with Paul to Paris and then to Amsterdam." He said the words quite distinctly and slowly to be sure she would understand, while at the same time emphasizing their meaning with his hands. After a summer in Tossa, his hands had acquired a vocabulary all their own when talking with foreigners. All four fingers would flap against his thumb meaning "talk," or he'd find himself pointing at whomever or whatever he was talking about. The habit had become so ingrained that sometimes he found himself doing it with English-speaking people as well.

"Margaret, she is gone. Now you go to Paris for Dominique." Nuria stated it like it was a matter of course.

"Perhaps," Brian countered. He leaned forward to give Max a pat on his side. "How was your summer, eh Max?" Max could only be bothered to toss a few lazy wags of his tail.

"His name no is Max. Is called Perdut."

"Perdut? Everyone calls him Max."

"What you know, *turista?*" she scolded, as if Brian were an ignorant child. "To the Catalan people he is Perdut."

The playful smile on Brian's face faded when he saw how serious Nuria was about this. "What does Perdut mean?" he asked, looking at Max as if for the first time.

"How do you say when you have no mother and no father?"

"An orphan."

"Yes," she nodded in agreement. "But in Catalan is more. Is different . . . it is how you say . . . lost. He haves nobody. He goes where is best for him. Now the summer is finished, he comes to me.

"*¡Oportunista!*" she cried, affectionately giving Max a brisk rub on his stomach. The King of Tossa's only response was to open his eyes long enough to wriggle into a more comfortable position.

"What will you do now that summer is over?" Brian asked. "Will you go away?"

"No, I am in Tossa. The Llibertat is open always." The pride of that achievement lightened the color of her dark eyes.

"Why do you not go around with the others in the summer?" His "sign language" armsweep took in the whole town. "You have no friends? Boyfriends? No *chicos?* I only see you work."

She gave only an unconcerned shrug. "I am Catalan."

"Yes, but you are too pretty, too beautiful to spend your whole life working in a little town like Tossa. Don't you want to know more of the world?" he demanded.

"You speak more slowly. I no understand."

He repeated himself.

"I wish to know the world," she said. "I no like Tossa so much, but I am Catalan and there is my mother. They both need me." She leaned forward to wrap her arms around her knees while she stared at the sea.

In the sun, crouched against her knees, she was, to Brian, a magnificent Asian idol with those half-slanting eyes. She was as desirable to him now as that first night he'd met her, even without the protective, soft lights of the Llibertat to hide the languor and thinness. But what he was drawn to most was the unshakable conviction in her voice. All of a sudden all he wanted was to feel like her: that something could be that right, that true.

The slap of the waves from the shore became louder and more demanding, as if the wind had picked up. Brian instinctively looked to check the pants drying on the clothesline running from the castle wall. But the trouser legs hung limp, showing no wind.

Then, looking out between the hulls of the two fishing boats in front of them, he spotted a freighter inching across the horizon. Finally the ship slid behind the castle and the quiet rhythm of the sea returned. Summer in Tossa was like that ship, he thought, gone without a trace, leaving no sound in its wake.

Inside he was growing angry. Why had he come here at all today? Why was he still in Tossa?

He turned back to Nuria, hoping to see in her sullen gaze the same troubling things, but the dark eyes had shifted their attention to where Marcello and Santiago were coming down the steps. The cousins trudged toward them in the sand. All they had for Brian was the same perfunctory nod that had greeted him all summer.

The machine gun stutter of their Catalan rattled in his ear for a few minutes. He envied the intensity of their conversation, despite not understanding a word of it. And then the three of them left, with only a curt farewell from Nuria.

Brian reread the letter from Dominique he'd received in yesterday's mail. She was to begin stewardess school today, that is if today were Wednesday. If you weren't a worker or a tourist on two-week holiday in Tossa, all the days seemed the same, unless, as Brian had joked with Ben once, "You can count how many days since the *supermercado* was last closed in the afternoon because that had to be a Sunday."

He didn't want to start this tormenting of himself again. He tried to think of something else. His girls this summer. Brenda. She must be in Morocco by now, he thought purposefully. All she wants is a quiet, respectable marriage, but she'll end up with some brawling pub-crawler. After their first night, she and Brian had only shared the boredom of waiting for summer to hit full stride, and he'd left her at first chance, like everything else in his life. Dominique was going to be a stewardess and see the world. Margaret was high above the Atlantic by now, on the way to begin that social work career she couldn't stop talking about. Everyone was going on to something. Everyone but him and Max.

Brian looked around the beach now empty of everything except the fishing boats. Yes, it was time to leave Tossa. Why wouldn't Paul hurry up and close for the summer? Suddenly he couldn't sit still. He was halfway up the steps when he called for Max to come. The King of Tossa opened his eyes and decided it was better where he was.

Brian came back to the small beach below the Llibertat the next day. He found Nuria lying in the same spot, with Max sleeping in the narrow strip of shade along her body.

"May I sit with you?" he asked.

She sat up to welcome him.

"How are you?"

"Good. It is cold today on the beach, yes?"

"Yes," he said. "Soon there will be no more beach."

"No, for me I come much times now. It is the best times with no peoples."

"There is a beautiful loneliness now that everyone is gone," he agreed, looking around. He could see from her puzzled expression she had not understood him. "A solitude," he added for clarity.

"Yes," she answered stiffly. "I understand."

In the days that followed, they would meet at the same place, with Max sometimes tagging along, and sit between the fishing boats for protection from the winds that sprang up in the shadows of late afternoon.

"You see your dirty air in Barcelona!" he snapped one day, feeling comfortable enough with her now to show anger. "Why are you Catalans trying to kill your beautiful country? Why do you refuse to learn from America's mistakes?"

"It is true. We are too commercial. All the times now Catalans think only of the money . . ."

Another time, looking at the cover of Brian's book, *The Outsider*, she said, "It is different between the two men. Sartre, he is a philosopher; Camus, he only asks the questions . . ."

One afternoon they watched Paul walking along the cliff.

"Paul does not know where he belongs," Brian told her.

"You are the same," she said with resignation.

"That is why he and I are friends . . ."

One time she began yelling at Brian. He could not remember her this angry before, but it was a part of her he liked. "You talk of American *cultura!* What do you know of *cultura, americano? Hamburguesas*, frisbees, big *coches*. There is my *Catalunya* two hundred years before *Cristóbal Colón* sees your Indians the first time."

The sun was lost one day without warning behind a wall of clouds that sprang up from behind the hills. "Today, we go to a special place," she said as they put on their shirts against the chill. She guided him along the water's edge to the far end of the beach, where a small cave bore into the base of the cliff. Nothing of the town was visible from the vantage point. Even the Llibertat, just above them, was hidden by the angle of the jutting cliff.

They climbed onto the small shelf of rock that served as a small porch at the entrance to the cave. Inside, Brian immediately felt the heavy cling of the trapped damp air. Unconsciously, Nuria moved closer to him. He took her hand for the first time, sensing her freedom now that they were out of sight of the Llibertat.

The cave was not very deep, ending not more than ten yards away where the ceiling sloped, too low for them to stand up straight.

"A whole summer here and I never knew this place existed," he marvelled, leaning back against the rocky wall.

She leaned back next to him. "I come here since I am a child."

"Alone?"

"Not all times. Sometimes with Marcello and Santiago until we have more years. Then I come alone. It is where I think. It is good with the sea all times close."

"This place is good. A place to run and hide from the world," he said, looking around it once more.

"It no is good like that. It is a good place only to think."

"But why do you always come alone now? You have no boy-friends."

She only stared down at the rust-colored rock floor.

"No boyfriends, ever? Why not, someone as pretty as you?" he chided.

"I am different," she murmured, raising her eyes to his to show him it was the truth.

Brian pivoted away from the wall to face her. "You mean you are Catalan."

She stayed glued to her place. "No, it is more than that."

He looked for the explanation in her eyes, but they were only a smoky mirror reflecting the light from the mouth of the cave. Their deep brown color was lost in the glare like the glazed stare of an animal blinded by a beam of light. He moved his head to shade her face. When he bent to kiss her, she closed her eyes and neutrally accepted his lips, absorbing the kiss without passion or protest, as if it were some strange gift she didn't know how to use. Brian pulled her closer to him, but she was stiff in his arms, like all the corpses he'd touched in the jungle.

"Why don't you want me to kiss you?" he whispered.

She said nothing.

"It means that I like you when I kiss you," he said. "I want us to be more than two people that lie on the beach and talk."

"It no is good." She stepped away from the wall.

"Why would it be no good?"

"You are leaving soon."

"I would stay because of you," he said, realizing how much the well-worn words reeked of seduction when, this time, it wasn't true at all.

She ran out of the cave and up the beach to where they'd been sunbathing. He caught up to her as she was picking up her towel. "Nuria, you and Paul . . . you are my best friends in the whole world. But you, Nuria, you are more than my friend. How do I get you to understand that? You still don't realize what you mean to me."

Max suddenly appeared from behind one of the boats.

"Perdut and you are the same," she said. "Today you are with me. Yesterday it is Margaret." She couldn't find a natural resting place for her hands, moving them about angrily. "Always like Perdut you go where it is best. Soon you leave Tossa for something better."

"You really don't believe that. Do you think I stay with you because there is nothing better?"

"You are just a *perdut*. You stay with me because all the other girls leave now when summer is finish. You will go. Like Perdut you only come to me when summer is over. You are both lost, but he is not in fault. He knows nothing more. You know other things. Why you no leave Tossa? Why you stay?" she cried, wiping her eyes with her towel.

"I stay in Tossa because of you! How can you not know that after all this time?" he said, but already knowing the words were useless.

"You will leave. This is no good!" She wouldn't look at him. "It is cold," she pouted, rubbing her elbows with her hands crossed in front of her. "I go now."

She was gone up the steps and out of earshot so quickly it was too late for Brian to do anything but stand there, watching the feline figure disappear inside the Llibertat.

As the church clock rang out the two-thirty chimes, Brian crossed the dark plaza with his hands jammed deep into his pockets to keep warm. The familiar walk up the hill to the Lliber-

tat seemed unusually long tonight. He especially missed the crowded outdoor tables of summer where you could always find a friend.

"Hi," Brian said awkwardly, once inside the Llibertat. He stood in the orange light, thankful Nuria was alone in the bar, making it worth waiting until this late in the evening after all. "Can we go out or must you stay open?"

"It is best I stay open."

He judged the lilt of her voice tenuous at best. Her uncertainty encouraged him to press on. "I want to talk to you."

"We talk here," she said, without much conviction.

"I want to talk to you where no one else will come to bother us," he said sharply, opening the front door for her.

She came out from behind the bar and followed him outside and down the steps of the cliff.

The beach was sallow in the weak glow of the lone street lamp on the castle wall. Tonight he was leading the way across the same route they had taken to the cave that afternoon. When they stopped at the mouth of the cave, Brian asked, "Are you cold?" She shook her head, but he knew she was, as was he. He cursed to himself because he had no better place for them to go. Maybe they should've stayed in the warm Llibertat, after all.

"I don't understand why you ran away from me this afternoon. Did I do something to hurt you?" he asked.

"It was nothing."

"You are right about me. I am a *perdut* with everyone . . . everyone except you. How do I make you understand that? It is so difficult to say these things because my Spanish is nothing." The chill from each breath knifed right through his lungs into the rest of his body. "All my life I have been a *perdut*. I learned it from my father. He taught me how to take what I wanted without paying the price. Do you understand what I mean?"

"Yes . . . I understand," she said hesitantly.

He spoke even more slowly. "All the other girls this summer, with them I am a *perdut* because I cannot find anything to want. But I cannot be like that with you. I feel different about you. What you want makes me love you."

"No, it is not possible for that. I am no good."

The desperation in her voice was lost on him on the empty beach. "You hardly let me touch you, but just being with you makes me feel even more alive than I did making love to all the others. You tell me about all these Catalan things you believe in. I

don't understand them, but it makes me feel maybe there can still be something for me too."

"It no is good for you and me," she said grimly. "We are different. I am bad."

"You are not bad for me. Just to be with you makes me feel good. It is enough to hold your hand."

"What do you know of bad!" she lashed out, clutching a lump of sand in her fist for revenge and then letting the grains slip through her fingers.

"I am worse than anything you could know, Nuria. What could be more evil than to kill someone for nothing?" he said, wanting to choke on the words.

She was now really hearing him for the first time since they'd left the bar. "If you do that, why you not in prison?"

"Because it was in the war and nobody knew about it except my buddy. And he's dead now too, killed in the war."

She did not flinch at the words as he'd expected, had hoped she would.

He went on, "I don't know why it happened. War makes you, how do you call it, *loco*. My buddy and I were on an easy patrol. Everyone was relaxed now that the gooks had been stopped. We stopped our jeep in the middle of a road. There was no reason to do it except to relax in the sun for a few minutes. We were sitting ducks like that, but it didn't matter. There was only this farmer working the field with his family, and the trees where snipers could hide were too far away. Nuria, you see . . . oh, how can I make you understand . . . baking in the sun like that with my eyes closed, it was like being home. . . . All of a sudden, Nuria, I really wanted to go home, not in the usual way, but so bad. I found I was crying. All I could see was this lousy country with its gook farmers and gook women and gook kids who hated me and I hated them.

"I shot him, Nuria." Brian had to look away as he said the words. "I shot him because it was his slimy stinking country that was making me so scared. I could die any minute and I didn't know why. I was killing people and didn't know why. I didn't know anything except killing because someone was trying to shoot someone else all the time. It had all gotten so easy it was like a natural part of your life. I just shot that poor farmer. . . ."

"You shot him." She put an imaginary rifle to her shoulder.

"And then the rest of his family ran. . . . Thank God they did because I swear I would've shot them too. I only meant to scare him . . . no, that's a lie. I don't know what I meant . . . that's the whole thing of it . . . life was so cheap . . ."

Brian tossed a few pebbles at the sea, listening for their insensitive "plunk" as they hit the water. "Shooting the farmer changed everything for me somehow. I couldn't shoot my weapon after that. I'd just fake it until I couldn't even do that and then they sent me back to the States. Battle fatigue, they called it."

"You would not want me if you know how bad I am," she said, moving closer to him.

"To me you cannot be bad. That we are together is all that matters."

"No, I am bad. You say the worse part of you but I still no can say to you the bad in me."

"Is that why you ran away today?"

"It was much things. It is that you are *un americano* and I am Catalan. I am here with *americano* when there is such important things in *Catalunya*."

"I don't understand."

"This morning my mother tells me my cousin is in prison. On the beach I think how crazy and bad it is I am with you."

"Which cousin? Marcello? Santiago?"

"A different cousin from Barcelona."

"Why is he in jail?"

"There is a *manifestación* and the peoples begin . . . you know," she pummelled the air with her fists.

"You mean a fight, a demonstration."

"Yes. They burn the *coches* at *la Facultat de Medicina*. They ask my cousin why he is there when his card say he is a student of the *filosofia*."

"But why arrest him?"

"Because he is *estudiant* of the *Filosofia* at *la Facultat de Medicina*," she said impatiently, as if it should be obvious to everyone.

"The card. You mean an identification card. They arrested him because he was a philosophy student."

"That is right. Only the *estudiant de Medicina* is permitted there because of the *manifestación* . . . demonstration. My mother say he will be in jail for much years."

"For being at the wrong school. How can that be!"

"The *Guardia* say all the peoples who no are *estudiantes de Medicina* are *revolucionarios*."

"Because of the demonstrations."

"*Sí.*"

"Did he burn the car?"

"He say no. It is the truth. He does nothing. Only looks with his eyes."

"Your family is always in trouble with the *Guardia*," Brian said, remembering Raoul's comment after the incident in the Llibertat that first night in Tossa.

"We are not *revolucionarios* in Tossa. Marcello and Santiago have only fights," she said guardedly. "My cousin who is in jail, he goes to many demonstrations. The police want him many times. Now they will have him in jail for seeing the *coches* burn, but it is the truth because he was in many other of the demonstrations."

"I didn't realize that so many people are saying things that are bad for the government."

"*¡Ay!*" she said disgustedly. "Here in Tossa you do not see it. The peoples are too busy making the money." She held up her hand, rubbing her forefinger and thumb together. "Tossa is not *Catalunya*. Tossa is *inglesa, alemana, francesa, holandesa*. It forgets it is Catalan. All *Catalunya* forgets it is Catalan. The peoples are rich from *los turistas*. They no care. Before, in the war they care. *Catalunya* is one of the last to fall to the *fascistas* because we are brave. Now we are very busy and no think of my father's *España*. To be rich makes *Catalunya* sleep like babies after the milk from their mother. The *estudiantes* in Barcelona speak. They want to show that everyone no is happy with *España*."

"You never see that. You never hear it."

Nuria smiled cunningly. "The government is very intelligent. When the government think there will be a demonstration like *la Fiesta del Primero de Mayo*, they have on the *televisión* many good things to keep the peoples home. There is *fútbol* and the *gran prix*. The peoples no come to the demonstrations. They are at home to see the *televisión*. Then the government can say is only a few crazy *revolucionarios*. Is nothing."

"Maybe that's true if the people don't care enough to come instead of watching football."

"No! No! The peoples only need the organization in *Catalunya* to make them not sleep. On the *televisión* they will never see that some of the peoples care. On the *televisión* the government shows all the problems in the world. Viet Nam for your people. The *comunistas* in Paris. Yesterday they tell us there is no food in Pakistan. But there is no bad news in *España*. *España* is always happy. *Todo son flores*, they say on the *televisión*. But many know the truth. The *vascos*, the Basque, do much. In *Catalunya* is necessary an organization to make the peoples think of *España* and *Catalunya*. Not money."

He felt shame that after all these weeks he still did not know her. "You are so young to think of these things," he said.

"I am not young," she said angrily. "My father kills *fascistas* in *la Plaça de Catalunya* when he haves nineteen years like me. He fight for what he know is good. Is that all finish? We lose the war, not our honor. He goes to *Francia* after Barcelona is finish, but he never stops the war against the *fascistas*. He *Resistencia*. Now is the time for the children of *Catalunya*."

Brian couldn't believe in this Catalonia thing of hers. It was happening too quickly and in too different a world. But he did believe in her and that was enough, even if her cause was no more right than Raoul's. Maybe her father was some glorious nineteen-year-old hero as she believed, killing for the right reasons; and then maybe, like Brian, he was just someone caught up in all the savagery through circumstances rather than cause. Either way made no difference because you had to become a beast to survive war. You ended up shooting just to stay alive, and everything else became lost in the process.

How could he tell Nuria about all this? Her father wasn't around to confirm it, but Brian was sure he would have. There were only a few years in age between Brian and Nuria, and yet the difference could not be measured in the days or weeks or months of the calendar. They were best measured by the senseless bullets fired, the men killed, the startled faces of a widowed family just before they turned to run for their lives. How could he ever explain all this to her? He only wanted to go inside the cave with her and hold and be held. In the dark, even without words, she would understand how lost and frightened he really was.

When, for the second morning in a row, I found my clothes were still damp from the night air, I knew it was definitely time to split from Tossa. The parade of gray days had come back and winter was beginning to comfortably settle into the old walls. The weekend Barcelona crowd had trickled to nothing. Except for Brian, George was the only regular still coming around the bar. I had only waited this long because of Brian. He was in some weird time warp, acting like a high school kid, not wanting to leave Nuria, content just to be near her fuzzy little muff.

George kept me company, drinking up the last of the D.Y.C. while I went around putting everything in order so I could leave the next day. That afternoon I liked George. There had been none of the spy bullshit ever since the old Spanish broad had moved in with him after she saw him pull out his fat roll of pesetas to pay for her drinks.

While I packed things away, George babbled on. "You can't believe how good it is to be able to talk to someone while I'm drinking, Paul. I'm going crazy out there. She doesn't speak English."

"Hmmm." I was too busy to really take an interest.

"You know how I forget my goddamn Spanish when I'm drunk. With her not speaking English it's like drinking alone. Paul, you know how I hate drinking alone. . . ."

"Want to kill the last of this bottle so I can throw it out?"

"D.Y.C.'s for horses, not for men; they say that it'll kill you, but they don't say when," he chortled, grinding out his pet verse as he offered his glass for a refill.

I smiled because I knew I wouldn't have to hear it again until next year. "I don't know how you drink this Spanish shit anyway," I said, filling his glass with the last of the bottle.

"The first few years my stomach cramped up after three or four shots . . . now it cramps up only if I have three or four." He let out his big horselaugh.

Brian came in the door, unusually early in the afternoon since he'd been seeing Nuria. For a moment, judging by his preoccupied gaze, I had the small hope they'd broken up.

"Hey, Brian. I'm glad I caught you," George said. "Maria and I are staying at Cala Salions all winter. Paul says you're staying too. Come see us."

Brian absentmindedly nodded to show he'd heard him. George went on talking until he'd finished his drink, and then left. We listened to his Mini take off down the street.

"You're back early. Something happen with you and Nuria?"

"Just a little fight. Nothing much. I'll go see her tonight and straighten it out."

I didn't want him to see my disappointment, so I busied myself with more packing. I'd hoped for a good last-night rap now that the bar was closed.

"This Nuria scene is nowhere, Brian. You know the trouble you can get into fooling around with her."

"I'm not fooling around with her," he protested. "I've been telling you, this is different. I haven't even kissed her."

"No one understands the weird family scene going on up there. There can only be trouble, Brian. Come to Paris like we planned!"

"I want to see it through."

"We've been talking about this trip for months," I pandered. "Paris has the greatest fox collection in the whole world and you're sitting here slowly getting prick-teased to death!"

"Let's forget it," he said.

"What about Dominique?" I knew that was a dirty trick, but it was really for his own good to get him out of there.

"I'm staying," he said stubbornly.

"Jesus, you're just like Bernardo. You both fall in love if they won't ball." Judging by Brian's glare I could see pushing the matter any further was like pissing into the wind. "So you're Nuria's first beau," I mused. "An American, no less. When I think of how Madeleine will react when she finds out. Why, to see that bitch pissed off, it's almost worth staying."

Brian shot me another angry look. "Ok, ok," I said, holding up my hands to ward off his angry stare. "I know you really like her. But I hope to Christ you know what you're doing." For the first time I was really worried. It wasn't just the hope of a dynamite ball that had kept him sniffing around Nuria's manhole so long. "Anyway, you can stay here. Just lock up and turn off the water when you leave," I mumbled.

"I never felt this way about anyone before," he said, almost apologetically.

"She is a fox," was all I could think to say. I popped the cap off my last cold San Miguel so hard the bottle burst open, drenching us both with beer. "Oh shit," I growled, shaking the foam off my sleeve. But Brian didn't seem to notice the mess. He was daydreaming about Nuria again.

The next afternoon we were both in front of La Vida waiting for my taxi to take me to the Gerona station. Brian listened impatiently to me drone out the instructions one more time. "You remember where all the water valves are?"

He rattled off the list again of how to close up the bar when he left. Impatience was creeping into his voice.

"And don't forget to unplug the fridge . . . leave the door open, otherwise it'll stink from mold," I said. There wasn't much else after that. I was happy as he to see the taxi working its way around the corner of the narrow street.

"You got Chris's address in Paris to find me?" I asked, so paternally it embarrassed me.

He nodded.

"I'm getting good at goodbyes," Brian said after we'd loaded my bags into the cab.

"Tossa gives you a lot of practice," I murmured self-consciously. Suddenly he'd caught me up in such a powerful hug it knocked me off balance. We held onto each other for the longest instant while the tireless valves of the taxi engine kept ticking away, impatient to be gone. I could only manage a feeble farewell. "Tossa goodbyes aren't supposed to be like this. See you soon . . . I hope."

Max stoically accepted my goodbye pat on the head. The brown eyes were already steeled up for the coming winter. Too many exhaust pipes of too many cars pulling away had hardened him to parting long ago.

"Don't forget to leave all the closet doors open too," I yelled for no good reason as the cab pulled away.

"Don't worry," he yelled back with an understanding grin about my foolish last-minute prattle.

I could see him and Max growing smaller and smaller in the rear window and then they were gone when the taxi turned the corner.

Tossa was like it always was when I left for the winter, with all the store windows shrouded in whitewash and the streets deserted. I was seized by this insane impulse to turn the taxi around and stay. It had nothing to do with Brian. It was only the temptation of the simplicity of wintertime Tossa, where the solitary days slip by so easily with no one to complicate your life.

The taxi stopped for cross traffic at the Gerona crossroads. A lone car heading for Barcelona was like an eleventh hour reprieve, offering me the opportunity to turn the driver back, but I said nothing. The car sped past us and we slowly pulled away, picking up speed past the last few white houses. Finally, the sign with the red slash through "Tossa" came by, marking the end of another summer.

We climbed over the ridge of hills and Tossa was left behind on the seaward side, floating away in the long flat plain of Catalonia that lay in front of me with all the sleepy villages that never saw a tourist all year.

Y ou are early this night," Nuria told Brian while she poured his beer.

"La Vida is closed now. Paul left for Paris today."

Madeleine was the only other person in the bar. Judging by her large glass of cognac and the French custom of lingering over their drinks, Brian knew she would be there for a long time.

"I looked everywhere for you after Paul left. Where were you?" he asked Nuria urgently.

"When Paul comes again?" she countered, ignoring his question.

"Nuria, I needed to be with you this afternoon." How could he make her understand his sudden hatred for the town today when Paul had left and he couldn't find her at any of their favorite afternoon haunts? To combat his loneliness he had walked up the coastal road, not stopping until long past dark when the hills along the sea were an anonymous black wall broken only by the warm lights of the town and the comforting clockwork sweep of the lighthouse beam.

"I can not see you tonight," she whispered.

"Why not?"

"It is necessary I stay with my mother." To avoid his eyes she busied herself, crushing out her barely smoked cigarette.

"Again," he hissed, stealing a glance at Madeleine to see if she was watching, which she was. "You spend a great deal of time with her. I want us to be together."

"I can not. It is necessary I am with her. She is lonely today."

"Can't you go out after she has gone to sleep? I need you too. Tonight I feel lonely." The last words had been so hard to say.

"She say she does not want me outside in the night. I think she know I am with you."

"She will have to know sometime." He was finding it hard to keep his voice to a whisper. "This is ridiculous. We live like school children."

"If I say it is you then she will finish it. We will not be together. It is very complicated," she said with a finality meant to put an end to the conversation.

This was the last straw for Brian in a day of increasing alienation. He had stayed for her, and yet they were barred from being with each other in this very room where they spent so much time together. They weren't even together when she was near him. There could only be the "accidental" brushing of thighs when she sat down next to him. She would not let him even briefly lay his hand over hers as they sat across the bar from each other. "It is because of my mother," was all she would explain curtly each time he'd asked why.

Tonight he had no room in his life for the frustrations of this same old sham dictated by something she would not explain. He angrily put the money on the bar for his barely touched beer and stormed out the door without another word.

Yes, Madeleine probably knew about them, and he was as helpless about it as if mired in quicksand. Every twist or turn only seemed to make things worse. In the plaza he glanced up at the church clock. It was edging toward eleven-thirty. He laughed to himself at the irony of the hour. It was the earliest he had ever gone home in all these months in Tossa.

Brian climbed the hill to the Llibertat many times the next day, looking for Nuria on the small beach. At last she was there, leaning against one of the boats, immersed in conversation with Marcello and Santiago. Nuria's greeting to Brian was even more aloof than last night's. The cousins only stopped talking long enough to give a tense nod of recognition. Feeling out of place, Brian dug small holes in the sand with his boot tip and then filled them up again while listening to their Catalan words.

Since Paul had left yesterday, Tossa had become as strange and foreign to him as the rest of Europe. Between his trips to the beach he had wandered from bar to bar, drinking coffees and beers just to kill time. He could find nowhere to belong in the whole town.

Marcello suddenly asked him, "You in Tossa all the winter?"

"I don't know. Perhaps," Brian replied, trying to seem strong. He looked at Nuria, who kept avoiding his eyes.

"Why you wish to be in Tossa for the winter?" Santiago probed, to the point of challenge.

Brian said nothing. The silence only encouraged Santiago further. His tobacco-stained teeth leered behind the bristly stubble. "You do not follow the girls north that you know in the summer?" he taunted, leaning back against an overturned fishing boat. "You very much please the girls here."

Brian felt the chill of the cold wind through his army jacket. Crazily, he reminded himself to buy heavier clothes for winter. He focused on Santiago's grimy teeth and said in an even voice,

"There were many nice girls here this summer. Didn't one or two like you?"

Santiago exploded into laughter. "Yes, there was a girl." The lips closed trap-like over the yellow teeth. "But now all times you are with my cousin."

Brian stiffened.

"Santiago!" Nuria cut in.

Santiago ignored her. "The summer in Tossa is good, Brian. I like it also. But with the Catalan women it is different."

"We are none of your business, Nuria and me."

Brian kept his gaze fixed on Santiago; for if it were to come to a fight, Santiago, not Marcello, would make the first move. Brian figured to hold his own with Santiago, if Santiago didn't go crazy and pull a knife or something like that. Still, there was Marcello. The bull could do him in without effort.

Suddenly Nuria stepped directly into Brian's line of sight. She turned her back to him, yelling at Santiago in Catalan and pointing to the steps. Santiago yelled back in an equally angry voice, and then turned to leave.

After a few steps he looked back at Brian. "I hope you leave Tossa soon," he warned, and then motioned for Marcello to follow him.

But Marcello made no move. "Nuria say you in the war. You are a soldier?" he asked innocently, as if the confrontation had not happened at all.

"I was once. No more," Brian answered guardedly.

"Is it difficult to kill?"

The sudden and sincere intimacy threw Brian into confused silence. When Santiago saw nothing more would be said, he tugged his brother toward the steps.

Brian watched them disappear from sight before grabbing Nuria's arm. "Did you tell them about me?"

"No. I tell nobody. I understand how it hurts you." She defiantly broke free of his grip. "I only say you are in the war. They wish to know." She tucked her arm against her side like a wounded wing.

"I'm sorry. I didn't mean to hurt you."

"Is nothing." She lowered her eyes.

"I'm upset today because you could not see me last night. I know that sounds foolish, but last night I needed to be with you. And this hassle with Santiago is too much. He thinks I'm not serious about you."

"He try to make my life for me because I am a Catalan woman. Do not listen to his words. I am *independiente*." She took his hand as proof of that. "I am sorry I could not be with you. My mother, she feels very bad. It is necessary I am with her."

"I don't understand," he said, thinking how often he'd said those words to her. "Is she sick?"

"No, it is the solitude."

"You mean the loneliness."

She let go his hand and retreated to the hull of the longboat.

He took the steps to bring them together again. "But what good are you to her?"

"We are together," she mumbled, barely loud enough to be heard.

He took her by the shoulders to keep them face to face. "You're talking around it, like you always do."

The wind had stopped, emphasizing her silence.

"God damn it, Nuria! Why won't you trust what we have together!" He let go of her. "Maybe you should've let it come to a fight with Santiago and Marcello. At least with them I understand why."

She began hesitantly. "You tell me you are bad. I tell you I am worse but you will not believe it. I am worse. I stop my mother from sadness."

"You're still talking in circles," he said wearily.

She lowered her eyes. Her voice turned girlish. "My mother and I sleep in the same bed."

Nuria raised her head when he did not answer. Suddenly the wind picked up again.

She burst out—"*Nous sommes lesbiennes!*"

It was the wail of a cornered animal, hanging in the air long after the words were gone.

She was crying. "How do I give myself to you now?"

He reached out to her, but she kept her distance.

"Now you know! I see how you are. I am ugly to you."

"No!" he cried. "It doesn't make any difference. If anything, I love you more for telling me. All I care about is if you love me."

"I love you very much. That is why I tell you. My mother is very lonely and sad when my father is dead. It is difficult for her in Tossa. I am all for her . . ."

"You don't have to explain anything."

"I wish to tell you. You are the first person I tell because you are the only one I wish to know."

"It makes no difference. How can I make you understand that?"

"You say that here, but if we are in the dark in our cave, and I tell you, it makes a difference. You would not touch me then."

"It would make no difference. You were very young."

"I am young no more. She cry, she tell me to stop, but we do it. You understand it is lonely for her with no one. I am still my father who she loves." She paused to catch her breath coming now in short bursts. "Before, I wish to do it with her. I wish to help her to be happy because I love her. But now I do not know what I am. I have the fear you will leave."

"That'll never happen."

She anxiously looked up toward the Llibertat. "I must go now."

"I will come to see you tonight."

"No, I tell my mother I stay with her."

"Nuria, I need you very much. I want to be with you no matter what has happened, but I can't share you this way. You have to make the choice."

"I must go," she repeated obstinately and left without giving him a chance to say anything else.

Watching her climb the steps he was only now beginning to comprehend Nuria's words, like when the pain of a gunshot wound finally defeats the body's first numbing defense. He tried like some voyeur to picture Madeleine and Nuria in bed. Women enmeshed in each other. He'd seen it in movies. Kisses, caresses, long oval fingernails skimming across hairless skin. But a film never came down off the screen into your lap. It always kept its distance from real life. Yet *it* happened in real life. *It! Say it! Lesbianism!* The word had never stuck before and now he was choking on it like some bone caught in his throat.

Nuria and Madeleine in the bedroom over the bar. The picture kept coming back to him. He had never seen their room, yet he'd always imagined it as square with a high, gabled ceiling. And now he furnished it with a bed and two fish swimming together, their fins moving slowly back and forth in an orange sea.

Why did Madeleine do it with Nuria? He must come to grips with that. It was the analytical part of him needing to know, always so uneasy without the answers. He could not say it was wrong. Who was he, a killer, to judge right or wrong? He hated Madeleine for taking away her daughter's freedom of choice about her life, but in a way he was shamefully glad because Nuria's secret was as terrible to her as his own was to him. The bond gave them a beginning.

Max stood up from where he'd been crouched in the doorway of La Vida when he saw Brian coming up the street. His sausage stub tail happily flopped back and forth. Brian was just as glad to see Max. Right now having the big empty house to himself would have been too much.

There was one bottle of *cacao* left in the bar which Brian gave Max as a reward for just being there. Max approached the drink a little more slowly than usual. A newly formed crust of dried blood was on his snout.

"A bad cat, eh! I guess we both had a bad day," Brian said with a rueful smile, while checking the wound. After Max had settled into his usual spot behind the bar, Brian started upstairs, very weary also of this day.

His bedroom on the roof terrace was cold now that the afternoon sun was just about gone. He lit the gas stove and lay down on the bed. As the stove heated up the room, the warm air was like a blanket pulling up over him. He was content to watch the clouds drift through the patch of sky in the doorway and listen to the hypnotic hiss of the gas stove.

He woke up wondering where he was. The world had turned into black, formless shapes. He realized it was evening. His body shivered from the cold, but he couldn't understand why it was so cold when the stove still hissed faithfully. Then he saw a patch of light behind the door, which must've been blown open by the wind. He reached for his shoe to knock the door closed, and then found Max's sleeping figure at the foot of his bed. It hadn't been the wind after all.

Max had never come upstairs to his room before. He'd always been content to stay in his corner of the bar or in the kitchen when it got too cold. But tonight he'd left the warmer two floors to be near someone. Some *perdut* he was. Even the King of Tossa needed someone.

Was Madeleine only reaching out too? To touch someone so she knew she existed, just as he had that night in Barcelona when he'd bought the whore because, as a stranger, he felt cut off from the warmth of the life going on all around him? Did Madeleine feel she was a stranger in Tossa? Being French, she was as different from these Catalans as these arid hills were from her lush, green France.

Suddenly Brian's image of her was more than that of a brooding stick figure at the end of the bar. Now Madeleine possessed the full kaleidoscope of human emotions: love, hate, passion, compassion, frigidity, joy, bitchiness. She became the woman who'd given up her own world to follow her husband back to his beloved Catalonia.

Brian switched on the light. The room was dreary in the glow of the single bulb. He lay there listening to the occasional creaks of the empty house intrude upon the hiss of the stove. Finally, he went out onto the terrace in restless disgust.

There wasn't even the barest trace of summer left in the whole town, none of the music and drunken laughter that would waft up from the street while he dressed each evening to make the round of bars.

His eye caught the postcard he'd left on the terrace wall more than a week ago.

> Back in Dusseldorf with my regular girlfriend.
> Summer is only a *geist* to me now.
> Bernardo

Bernardo had once said how when he got back to Germany he couldn't remember the names of his Tossa girls anymore. Even the childish Bernardo knew when summer was over. *When I was a child I spake as a child. . . . Now that summer is over I put away my childish things.* Brian thought maybe he should leave Tossa, as well.

He crossed the terrace to look down into the same predictable silence of the other street. It was loneliness that was seducing him into leaving Tossa now and roaming again as he always had. Loneliness. The same shark that had made Madeleine in her own human terror devour her daughter. Now he really understood the frescoes from the last days of Goya's life he'd seen in the Prado . . . especially the one called *Child Devoured by Satan.* Loneliness had conquered Goya too . . . a Goya of gaiety and triumph reduced in his old age and blindness to the despair of painting the absolute, pitiful nights of existence.

The night outside became oppressive to Brian. He went back indoors. Max couldn't take all his stirring about, so he callously departed down the steps. The final desertion, Brian thought. He started to call Max back, but changed his mind. He switched off the light to lie in darkness again.

He wouldn't go to Paris. He must see this thing with Nuria through if he'd meant any small part of what he'd told her. Wasn't his love real enough to endure loneliness? Today it was, but tomorrow would he run from loneliness to isolation again? He'd always conquered loneliness by finding someone to share it. But sharing was different than loving. He'd never known real loneliness until now, now that he'd lost Nuria. The hypnotic hiss of the stove began closing in again, making him feel very tired. . . .

The creak of the door awoke him. He sat up. The silhouette in the doorway froze at his sudden movement.

"Who is it?" he whispered.

"I am sorry I wake you," was the whispered response.

"Nuria?"

"I think I make little noise."

He squinted at the luminous dial of his watch. "What time is it?"

"It is late."

"How did you get in?"

"The door is open to the street." She waited for her eyes to adjust to the darkness of the room before coming over to him. The bed creaked when she sat down. "I come to be with you," she said softly. He could feel the cold from her body now that she was near him. "On the beach you say I have to choose. I do not know what I want. I tell my mother this night I no stay with her. She cries. It no pleases me to hear it. I come here. But her *melancolía* is in my head now with you."

"I love you, Nuria, no matter how it is." He kissed her.

She let his lips touch hers for only a moment, and then pulled back.

"Brian, it is not good like this. I no can sleep with you."

"It's not important to me." He meant it for the first time in his life.

"You wish to know why."

"You don't have to say anything."

"I no make love with you. I no want to do it."

"It only matters we are together."

"You will not be sad if I go back to Madeleine?"

"Any time we have together is enough," he said, understanding for the first time the beauty of lovers dying together.

She did not move in his arms for a long time. Then he shifted to stop the cramp beginning in his arm where he'd cradled her head. She stirred at his movement. "I woke you this time. I'm sorry," he said.

"I am not sleeping. I think of my father. Much times in the night I think of him. He was very brave in the war. When the *fascistas* gain Barcelona, he goes to Vich to make the last fight of *la República*. It was very bad for them. The army haves little bullets and food. They leave Vich when it is all gone and run to the town of Nuria in the mountains. It is a little village near *Francia*. "You know of it?" He didn't. She continued, "My father tells me it is very cold there. There is only snow to eat. My father loves Nuria. It is the last place of *España* he sees before he goes over to *Francia*. That is why he calls me the same.

"In the *Resistencia Francesa* he kills many *Boche*, and when the war is finished they say he is very brave. But the war makes him old and sick.

"He always tells my mother and me, all he wish is to die in *Catalunya*. He say, 'Nuria, you are Catalan, not *francesa*, remember that all times. People is like their earth,' he say to me. 'In *Francia* all is green and soft. The people of *Francia* are not hard. That is why they fall to the *Boche* so quick. In *Catalunya* we fight much years against the *fascistas* with not so many guns and airplanes because we are hard and strong like our little trees that live in the dry hills.' My father say it is necessary for Catalans to be like the trees and be strong. But he is very sick in the heart when he sees the people. No one care no more. They have forgotten *la República*. My father is like a tree again in the earth after it is not there a long time. He dies but—" she choked even though she had thought these words so often. "He is in Tossa when he dies . . . his *Catalunya*. That is good even if he no gains the war."

"That is why you stay here?" Brian wanted to know.

"I am Nuria. Like my mountain I am the last of *Catalunya*. I stay to help my country." Even in the dark he could sense the prideful look on her face. "Young people. Now they begin to care. The old are tired . . . and rich. They forget *Catalunya*." She turned so that she was looking at him. "Tonight is special. I never feel like this with no one except my father. You are much like he, Brian. He was always alone, but he was no *perdut*."

"I am no *perdut* now."

"You do not change that easy," she said. "You are a *perdut* much times, but it no is important to me."

The first light of day appeared in the doorway. "I must go before the morning comes. It is still *España* . . . and I am *catalana y católica*," she explained, leaving his bed. "Tomorrow, come to the *supermercado* at two in the afternoon. I take you to a special place."

They walked down the Gerona road past the women doing their laundry in the little creek that deserved its name Tossa River only after a heavy rain. The creek parted from the road, and Nuria bade him follow her upstream, putting them out of sight of everyone. Using an old board for a bridge, they crossed at a narrow spot into the thick woods on the opposite bank. In this dense foliage, the open terrain of rolling hills and sea they'd just left seemed impossible to Brian.

The path began to climb along the slope of the hill. Here the woods quickly thinned out and only the squat cork trees survived, their limbs gnarled by the wind and their trunks stripped of their precious bark as high as a man could reach. Further up the hill the cork trees disappeared, leaving just scrub brush and rocks to anchor the soil. At the crest of the hill, the path circled back to the seaward face, and Brian could see Tossa in the distance, curled around the cove like an insignificant smear of white paint left on a seascape.

Nuria sat down, leaning back against a piece of the huge granite rock that formed the top of the hill. "My father bring me here many times. This is the last place he see Tossa before he goes to the war. This *vista* is with him all times. He tells me much times of his dream for *España*. In *la República* before the *fascistas*, the land is for the peoples. We come here and he say, 'Nuria, I give you my *vista* of *Catalunya*. It is all I have, *la meva filla*, my daughter.' It was to be like this . . ." she said regretfully, scanning the empty horizon. "It was to be good for all the peoples . . . the land with no barriers.

"In the summer when Tossa changes, I come here. Look there." She pointed in the direction of the hills. "It is still *la Catalunya auténtica*, yes?"

Brian followed her finger over the farms and houses scattered below. In his mind he became her father, exposed to the wind, taking one last look at the beauty he loved enough to risk his life for. This final memory was all he would have to carry him through the doubts and the nightmares of war. Was it worth it? He would have to keep telling himself something had to be spent to buy dreams. In every generation, some warriors die, some are wounded, and the rest stumble. But all are marked by war, and Brian wished he could be in the ranks of those who thought their scars worthwhile.

"Brian, you love me as you say yesterday?" she asked with an urgency that startled him out of his daydream.

"You know that."

"I need you to help me."

"Nuria, after how I've said I love you, do you think there is anything I wouldn't do for you?"

"You say that *muy rapidamente*. There is danger what I wish."

"You make it sound like you want me to kill." Everything was becoming too real too fast.

"I never ask you that. I know killing is the one thing . . . oh, it is too complicated for me to say," she cried out as her face grimaced with the frustration of the strange language. After she'd collected her thoughts she went on. "You say the truth when you say you know of the drugs?"

"That's it." He was so relieved it was not something serious after all.

"You know of *la cocaina?*"

"Nuria, you and the white lady!" He had expected her to ask about any drug except that one; even heroin would not have surprised him. "Coke's a heavy fall everywhere," he said.

"I no understand."

"It is as bad to be caught with cocaine as heroin. You go to jail for a long time if you're caught with cocaine."

"It is important to me and Marcello and Santiago to know about this cocaine. Will you tell them of it tonight?"

"Can't you tell them?"

"It is best we are all together."

"You know they don't like me."

"That is why it is difficult to ask you. But it is important to me."

He looked down at the adjoining hill, shamefully excavated into a campground. It was nothing but bare earth, except for a few remaining pieces of trash left by the summer tourists. "I'll come," he said, thinking how much like that hillside his life had become.

The Llibertat was deserted when he arrived. Without Nuria, the bar seemed new and strange, making him edgy. Still, he was glad not to have to face Madeleine. He was sure his face would betray his knowledge of her secret.

When Nuria came to the archway from the back room, Brian felt stupid for being so nervous. Nuria held her hand out to him. "Come, we sit with the fire."

He followed her into the back room where Santiago and Marcello were already seated.

"Hello, Brian." Marcello rose stiffly from his chair to shake hands.

Brian tried to fall in with the pumping rhythm while watching Santiago still standing noncommittally at the end of the fireplace. Brian pulled a chair up to the fire.

"Nuria," said Marcello. "Whisky, *si us plau*. Brian, I pay you a drink."

Brian really wasn't in the mood for drinking, but asked for a beer, not wishing to start the night on the wrong foot by refusing Marcello's hospitality.

"We have cold tonight. Winter is here soon," Marcello offered plaintively to the fire. "I go on the boat tonight."

"Where are you going?" Brian asked, going out of his way to seem interested even though he wished they'd get on to the real reason for the meeting.

"Fish," Marcello said with a look of distaste on his face for the coming task. "Summer is *kaput*. The fish is necessary for money."

"Santiago, you go with him?" Brian asked purposely to draw the other cousin into the conversation.

"Yes," Santiago offered grudgingly, shifting his weight, as if he too were impatient with the small talk.

"Is it difficult to catch fish?" Brian said to no one in particular and because he could think of nothing else to keep the conversation going.

"It is easy," Marcello went on, happy he could follow the conversation with his poor English. "With the light in the water the fish comes like insects. We are in the boats." He brought his huge hands together in the shape of the enclosing circle the boats made with their nets. "It is much work, but it no is difficult."

Nuria came back with the drinks. "Brian no is here to speak of fish."

"I know," Santiago said, obviously glad to get down to business. He sat down next to the others, offering his cigarette pack around the room before taking one for himself. "I wish to like you, Brian, because of Nuria. But you are summer *turista*. You ask why it is right for me to be with your *chicas* and you are wrong to be with a Catalan *chica*. There is no reason except I am Catalan. It is *la cultura*," he explained fatalistically. He drew on his cigarette pensively.

"Perhaps it is difficult for me because you are summer *turista*. Summer is good to us. We make much money. But in the winter you go to your home; for us there is still the *fascistas.*" Anger suddenly came over him. "It is more. It is the winter for *Catalunya* in here!" He brought his clenched fist to his heart and took a drag off his cigarette to calm down. "Nuria tells me you know much about the drugs."

"Some."

"For us it is very important."

Brian picked up the fire poker to free a nail from a burning piece of scrap lumber in the fireplace. He could feel the old familiar knot tighten in his stomach. He pushed the rusty nail back into the smoldering beam. It would survive the fire anyway.

"What can I do for you, Santiago?"

"You Americans are all the same, very direct," Santiago said with a grin.

"It's one of our few virtues."

"We Catalans are like the *españoles.* We do much for appearance. Pardon me for that. I am like this because what I ask you is dangerous for all here. Perhaps more dangerous for you because you are *un extranjero.*"

"No! He is no *extranjero!*" commanded Nuria, taking his hand to prove her point. "He is with me now all times."

Santiago ignored her melodramatic gesture. "We wish you to teach us about the drugs and to shoot the guns." He made the request as if it were a formal proposal at a negotiation.

"Is that all!" Brian sighed with obvious relief.

"It is more than you think. Not guns for shooting animals . . . but like you use in a war."

The knot in Brian's stomach drove a cramp through his bowels. He leaned forward to ease the pressure, hearing the growl in his intestines. "You mean machine guns and automatic weapons."

Santiago nodded. Brian's hand slipped unconsciously from Nuria's grasp. He returned to prodding nervously with the poker. He found the nail again while everyone watched, and pulled it away from the fire. "You have guns now?" he asked, still playing with the nail.

"We will have them soon."

"Why do you want such guns?"

"It is best you do not know."

"He is to know everything. We are one!" Nuria ordered.

Marcello ranted at her in heated Catalan. Her retort was even stronger until she caught herself and barked, "Speak English. If he is with us he has the right to know all."

Marcello threw up his arms in disgust. "Talk to her, Santiago."

Santiago remained silent; Brian, as well. He realized Santiago was only the leader in outward appearances. Nuria was their spiritual heart. The unbreachable faith he loved was the same reservoir for her cousins also. It was more than marvelous, it was an extraordinary thing at the very least in this *macho* Spanish culture.

"Brian," Nuria said, taking command of the situation. "All of us, we wish to fight the *fascistas* like the Basques. *Catalunya* sleeps too long times now. We wish for *Catalunya la independencia.*"

"Nuria . . . that's revolution."

"No, it is *llibertat.*"

"Just the three of you," Brian said in derision.

"It is a commencement. There will be more peoples when they know we exist. If not, we go to the Basques. They wish all peoples who have the guns. We make the *Catalunya* my father say to me . . . the *Catalunya* I dream."

"Nuria . . . your dream is only killing. I've had enough of that."

"Brian, this is not America. There is no equal election. You tell me on the beach the black peoples must take their equality. The white peoples in America will not give it without violence. It is not right, you say, but it is the only way for the black peoples. For us it is the same. *Todo son flores in España.* You remember? It is necessary to wake our peoples. I no ask you to be a soldier and kill. I only ask you to teach us of the guns."

"And then you leave me. Is that it?"

Her dark eyes turned hard, shining in the firelight. "My father leaves the peoples he loves because it is necessary. It is the same hour for the children of *Catalunya.*"

Listening to Nuria, Brian realized he had never won her from Madeleine because she had never really belonged to her mother. She belonged only to this insane dream. He was more jealous of *this* rival lover than anything because there was no way to defeat it.

"Guns are not easy to obtain," he said without much conviction.

"We buy them."

"They cost a lot of money," he argued. And then it all fell into place in his mind. "Of course, the cocaine."

"You know of that?" Santiago looked to Nuria, who nodded.

"Just that," Brian said.

"There is a man, a Catalan in Barcelona, who will sell us a kilo of *la cocaína*," Nuria explained.

"A kilo!" Brian's yell was a cry from out of his drug dealing past, when the possibility of a big score created an excitement that went beyond the money involved. "Do you know what that's worth on the street?" he clamored.

"No, that is why we ask you. How much is the value?" Santiago asked.

"If it's uncut . . . a lot!" Brian went on, caught up in the fervor.

"He brings it on the boat from South America."

"A million pesetas, easy," Brian said out loud, doing the figures in his head once again to check the conversion from dollars. "You trade these for guns?"

"No, we sell the cocaine to a man and with the money we buy the guns." Santiago looked to his shoes before going on in a lower, more humble voice. "Brian, we know nothing of this cocaine. Can you teach us of it?"

"I can't teach you without some. It is complicated for such large quantities. There are many ways he could cheat you."

The unexpected answer set Santiago back. He had been ready with arguments for a flat refusal.

Suddenly Brian said, "I can come with you and check it."

"You say that quick. It is dangerous."

"No more than the guns are for you."

"Remember, we are not fanatics. The *revolucionarios* of America were not fanatics. It is the same for us. We want the land for the peoples. I only ask you to teach us to use the guns and to tell us if the cocaine is *auténtica*. If you do not help us, we learn some other way . . . perhaps more dangerous."

"I said I would help you. I meant it."

Santiago went to get his coat. "We must go to the boats. We talk more of this tomorrow."

Brian could hear the front door opening and closing as Nuria let them out. *Guns and killing!* This had to be a dream, all this insurgency being planned in Tossa with life-and-death stakes. Or was the dream he and Paul and the rest of the family so easily tripping through summer, when the problems of a good suntan and the next piece of ass were all that mattered?

Nuria sat down next to Brian. He looked at her. Without her cousins, she seemed a very vulnerable and unlikely warrior.

"You don't know what it is to kill," he said. "You think it's romantic and will make everything good. All it does is make you an animal."

"Do not think we are children," she fired back. "I understand how much serious is this we ask you. Brian, I love you but always in my heart is that I must fight for *Catalunya*."

There was nothing he could think of to say against this thing that would take her away from him. She was as pure as the history she believed in, and what could ever defeat that?

"I don't believe in this Catalan independence," he said. "I don't know anything except what you tell me. It's crazy to me, even if you are right. Guns and death are not the way."

The lure of the fire was entrancing, but he quickly made up his mind. "I am not Catalan. It is not my country, but I believe in you, Nuria. You are the one thing in this world I believe in. I will help you because it is what you want."

Summer had ended forever as he said those words, but there were no regrets. He felt more alive inside than ever before, and something had to come of that.

Still groggy from sleep, Brian climbed aboard the early morning bus for Barcelona accompanied by Santiago and Marcello. The three men shuffled to the rear where they had the back seat all to themselves. Brian took the corner, waking from a doze each time a curve in the winding road bounced him against the window or Santiago. Giving up on the prospect of any more sleep, Brian asked, "Tell me about this man we are going to see."

"I know nothing about him," Santiago said.

Brian was stunned. "You don't know him and we're going to him for cocaine!" he whispered in amazement.

"It is no problem," Santiago said in a reassuring voice. "He is a friend of my cousin. The one who is in jail. The man we go to see is a *marinero* on a boat from South America. He brings the cocaine for us. He sells to us for the same price he buys it in South America because he is Catalan too. But to be safe we wish you to see it and tell us if it is *auténtica*."

"Where do we see him?"

"His pension."

"Who will you sell it to for the money for the guns?"

"A man who lives in Paris. I meet him in the Llibertat in the summer. He is called Julien. You know of him?"

"No. Who will take it across the border into France?"

"Marcello and me," Santiago said quite casually, sliding down in the seat to catch a short nap now that the road had straightened out. Brian looked to the other brother for confirmation, but Marcello had dozed off too, leaving Brian to watch the dull landscape of factories and highrise buildings that marks the approach to Barcelona.

The old building where the seaman lived, with its long stairways and dim halls, looked like all the other pensions in Brian's travels. No one was at the reception desk, so they were forced to find their way to the right room without any help. All for the best, Brian thought. The fewer people who saw them the better.

The seaman's room was at the back of the building. The man who let them in, dressed in a suede jacket and slacks, would've looked ordinary enough to Brian, except for the fact he was supposed to be a seaman. But Brian couldn't sustain his suspicions after the stranger said something in Catalan.

Santiago answered and, when the seaman shook his head, looked apologetically at Brian. "He speaks no English."

Brian went to the window. The courtyard below, walled off from the street noise by the surrounding buildings, afforded quiet privacy. The only sign of life was laundry drying on a clothesline. Satisfied there was no one nearby, Brian said to Santiago, "Let's get this over with."

The seaman sat down on one of the twin beds. Idly, he stepped on a cockroach scurrying across the no man's land between the two beds and swept the dead bug under the bed with his foot, muttering something which made the brothers laugh. Santiago translated for Brian. "He say the room is good value because you get the insects for no extra money."

"Where's the cocaine?" Brian urged. "Santiago, it's no good to waste time like this."

"I am sorry. It is the Catalan *cultura* again. *¿La cocaína?*" he asked, turning to the man.

That one word lit up the man's face with excitement. He gestured for Marcello to hand him the small suitcase on the chair. He placed the bag in front of him on the bed and unzipped a side pocket. The plastic pouch he presented was filled with a white substance that looked as innocuous as soap powder. Brian winced to himself at the amateurism of displaying the whole stash this soon. This novice move compensated for his own disadvantage of the language barrier.

"I'll need a sample," he told Santiago, who handed him the pouch. Brian had purposefully not eaten or drunk since dinner the day before, in order to get a good reading on the cocaine. He had snorted cut cocaine numerous times, but had only tried the pure, uncut form once in his life. Still, that one time had been enough to always remember the experience. These white chunks had the same luster when turned to the light. He sniffed a little off the corner of his fingernail and waited for the memorable rush. All three Spaniards sat watching him. The freeze hit his nostrils and front teeth at the right time, gently enough so that he was sure this was not some other anesthetic laced with speed to pass as cocaine. The rush to his head was just right too. Subtle, not heavy. "A good stone. It's dynamite merchandise, Santiago."

"What is the price to us?" Santiago asked in Catalan.

"It will go for the cause?" the man asked.

"We will buy guns with the money."

"The American will sell the cocaine?"

"No, he is with us."

"An American?" The seaman showed surprise.

"What does it matter?" Santiago snapped abruptly.

"You have many in your group?" the man inquired with interest.

"No, there is only us to begin. Let us finish this," Santiago groused, as he beckoned to Marcello for the money.

At that moment Brian was happy about the language barrier. It left him alone to enjoy the euphoria of the drug beginning to rush to his head.

"A pity there is only you. More would have been better," the seaman muttered while he reached into his suitcase. Santiago paid no attention to the comment or the seaman's movements until it was too late. Suddenly they were all looking at the same kind of pistol as the *Guardia* had pointed at Max. "You are under arrest for treason and drug possession," the man recited coldly in Spanish.

It's a ripoff for the money, was Brian's first thought at the sight of the pistol, not understanding the conversation. The high in his head throbbed insistently. All action seemed impossible, yet somehow he managed to raise his hands. The cousins confusedly looked at him and followed suit. They were too far away from the gun at this point to do anything else.

"It's a joke. You want more money for the cocaine?" Santiago asked weakly in Spanish.

"I am *Guardia Civil.* Your seaman friend is dead, in the closet. I was waiting to see who would come to buy his cocaine. How do you know him?"

When none of the three said anything the agent shook his head. "No matter. You three have never been in trouble as agitators, as you say?"

"What difference does it make?" Santiago said, disgusted because now he would have to endure the most horrible of all fates for their dream—stopped before they'd even begun.

The agent seemed pleased about Santiago's reply, as if it had been the cue for his next move. "I could arrest you as a dangerous *grupúsculo*. It would be good on my record, but it does nothing for my bank accout. Your dead friend will satisfy my record."

His voice changed to a friendly tone. "I am sure we can work something out. You should not have to pay so heavily for such a tiny mistake as buying cocaine. I give you this choice. Arrest for treason and drug possession or . . ." The agent paused, looking closely at each of them. "You may walk out that door. Without the money, of course."

Santiago's upraised hands twitched at the unbelievable words. "Why am I surprised?" he said, laughing to himself. "Why not the *Guardia Civil* too?"

The agent continued to eye them both calmly, showing no sign of guilt or hesitation. It was obviously not his first time in this situation. "One could even say I am doing my duty to my country by taking your money. Then you cannot buy guns."

"Why should we pay? If you arrest us, we will tell them all about this," Santiago challenged, but already knowing the answer.

"Who would believe Catalan terrorists?"

Santiago said nothing.

"Make up your mind. What will it be?"

None of them made a move, but the agent was not worried. Sometimes it was like this. "I could just as easily kill you and take the money," he reminded them.

All this time Brian had been fighting to keep his nervous system under control as the effects of the cocaine raced through his body, intensified by the anxiety of not comprehending what was happening. He had understood only a few words—*Guardia Civil*, cocaine, money. "He's the police?" he asked.

"*¡Hable español!*" the agent ordered.

"*Él no habla español. Es americano,*" Santiago answered forcefully to show they were not beaten yet. The agent ignored the challenge. To be safe, he signalled with his gun for them to face the wall.

Santiago moved toward the wall, and the others followed. Santiago saw no need to discuss the agent's offer with Marcello or Brian. To leave without their hard-earned money meant no guns—a fate as terrible as arrest.

"If we resist, he can only kill one of us," Santiago whispered in English.

"*¡Silencio! ¡Hable español!*" ordered the agent again as he started to search Marcello.

"Yes, Brian?" Santiago whispered.

"I don't know."

"Marcello, you understand . . ."

Out of the corner of his eye Brian could see Marcello whirl around to grab the agent. Brian mentally braced for the sound of the coming shot that was instead a dull metallic click. The struggling agent suddenly looked small with Marcello's hands around his neck. Marcello's bullish strength made killing a man look like nothing more than wringing the neck of a chicken. The agent could only manage choking gurgles in his desperate fight for air. He started to raise his pistol, but Marcello yanked him off his feet; with no floor for support, the fear froze his arms straight out, preventing him from taking aim.

Then Marcello flung the terrified man against the bed, which lurched with a hideous squeak when his neck smashed across the brass foot rail. The stiffened arms wilted as the agent slid to the floor, and then the head flopped forward lazily. Marcello hauled the dead man to his feet and draped him over the bed rail with his legs dangling in a slow *danse macabre.*

All three silently watched this bizarre pendulum movement.

"It is best," Santiago finally said. It was what everyone was thinking. But like the others, he could not look away from this first victim of their revolution.

Since the struggle, Brian had not moved except to lower his hands. Death had killed his cocaine high and brought him to his senses. "What do you think?" he said, finally moving over to the cocaine and stuffing the pouch into his pocket.

"I am not certain," Santiago said.

"Did he know who was coming, our names?"

"No," Santiago said, glancing over at Marcello. From his brother's expression he knew he was waiting for him to tell Brian of the attempted shakedown. Instead, Santiago said quickly in Spanish, "Not a word to him. Or Nuria."

"If there were others watching they'd have been here already,"

Brian reasoned. He looked to Santiago to find fault with his logic. "No one saw us come in. Let's leave and take our chances."

"Wait!" Santiago said as the idea came to him. Remembering the agent's words he opened the closet.

"What the hell . . ." Brian said when he saw the dead seaman.

"I'll tell you later," Santiago said, positioning the two men to look as if they'd killed each other in a struggle.

"It may not fool them, but it's worth a try," Brian said when the dead bodies finally looked right for the story. They wiped for fingerprints everywhere they could remember, and then slipped out of the building unseen.

The street scene was normal. Marcello started to hail a taxi, but Santiago pulled his arm down. "No, we walk. No one must remember us here." They made their way the few blocks to the long line of waiting taxis in the Plaza de Cataluña.

The taxi driver turned to make sure he'd heard the address right. "*¿Tossa de Mar?*" he repeated incredulously.

"*Sí, Tossa de Mar. ¡Vámonos, vámonos!*" Santiago confirmed. Then, speaking in English to the others, "There are always so many taxis here it is impossible to remember us."

Up to now they had been guided by their instincts. The taxi ride was the first real chance to think. Brian said there was no doubt the *Guardia* would come looking for the agent when he didn't report in. Still, as Santiago reasoned, no one had seen them, and the dead seaman hadn't known them. That was their edge. The only risk was their cousin in jail who knew the seaman. But there was no doubt the seaman knew others. And he was a smuggler. In any event, Brian was in the clear, having no contact with the family that would make him a suspect. All three decided that if anyone asked, they had ended up on the morning bus to Barcelona by coincidence and had decided to share a taxi back to Tossa instead of waiting for the evening bus.

It was all worked out by the time they reached the last few kilometers between Lloret and Tossa. Brian tried to enjoy the twisting road, but the image of the dead men would not go away. How much killing was worth staying out of prison, he kept asking himself.

It had been raining since they left Barcelona, making the taxi hot and stuffy with the windows closed. Suddenly Brian could stand the closeness no longer. He yelled at the driver to stop and threw the door open before the cab could even pull off the road.

Brian knelt in the mud and cursed all existence between agonizing waves of dry heaves that rendered him senseless. But still the faces would not go away.

"*¿Qué pasó?*" the driver asked his other two passengers as he watched the doubled-up figure vomiting in the rain.

"*Se enfermó*," Santiago said, looking annoyed. "*El camino.*" He wriggled his arm, meaning the curves.

The following week there was no news of the killings on the television or in the newspapers. It was as if nothing had happened. The only difference in Tossa was that the *Guardia* was now checking papers at the Gerona crossroads. But the Catalans, as always, showed identification without question or concern.

"It is not even certain this is because of the agent," Santiago told Brian. "Many things happen in *España* that we do not know."

To be safe, Brian hid the cocaine in Nuria's cave.

"It will bring much money?" Nuria asked as he buried it in a jar behind a rock where the ceiling sloped too low for him to stand upright.

"Yes."

He gave the makeshift vault one last look, praying the container would remain watertight.

"Brian, I did not want this for you."

"It was my doing. I'm not sorry. I'm inside at last."

"Marcello say nothing. He always have the dead man in his head."

"He will be ok. It just takes time."

"You are right about the killing. I do not see it, but I feel the blood too. It stains us all. Sometimes—"

"Don't you start thinking like that. It's your belief that holds me together."

"I will not change. It is just everything is so different."

"Nothing's changed. The danger just came early, that's all."

"You would make a good *general*," she said with a smile and patted his arm.

"Should we have some of that cocaine?" He knew that would keep them cheerful.

"No. It is bad."

"It's not, Nuria."

"It is only for the guns," she admonished him.

He grew angry. *The guns.* Everything was chattel to pay for the damn guns: their lives together, the man in jail, even the dead agent who would forever be nameless to them as well as to his nation. It didn't seem fair to Brian that in a culture where pride and bravery meant so much, a man could die ignominiously by a stroke of lousy luck while performing the dangerous job of protecting his country so well.

No one ever came to question any of them, and one day the *Guardia* just disappeared from the crossroads. The four sat as if strangers to each other in the Llibertat for a few more days, keeping their contacts to a casual minimum. And then one night after the last customer had left, Brian said, "I will take the cocaine to France. It's the best way."

"We cannot let you do that. You have done too much already. This is our war!" Santiago protested.

"It may be your war, but I'm in the middle of it."

"You have done much for *Catalunya* already." Santiago squeezed Brian's shoulder with affection.

"I don't do this for your Catalonia or your Spain. I want to do it for Nuria, and for you too. I could never have killed that man. If Marcello had not moved, we'd be in jail now."

"Brian," Nuria said. "We want no more from you. It no is right."

"If it had been *right* we would be dead instead of that agent!" Brian cried. "It's crazy you've lasted this long. You're lucky they didn't connect us to your cousin in jail. It's only incredible luck you're this close to your damn guns. The hardest part is still to come."

"It is our responsibility," Santiago said.

"How will you get the cocaine into France?" Brian prodded.

"I do not know," Santiago grumbled. It vexed him to have Brian probe at the same problem that had been troubling him.

"In a suitcase," Brian suggested.

"Perhaps. Maybe over the mountains."

"That's craziest of all! Only professional smugglers who know police routines do that. Think! The police may know there was cocaine. They must consider the possibility it was Catalans who were to meet your man. The agent did say it was for the cause, right? They will be suspicious if you disappear. They will search you at the border very thoroughly and the French will too, because they hate the Spanish coming into their country."

"It is a chance we take."

"As a tourist, they will pay little attention to me at the border. But two Catalans going to France right now . . . Be smart." Brian looked at the three of them, hoping for the slightest sign of agreement. Seeing none he went on. "Ok, say you do get to Paris, Santiago . . . None of you have ever used coke. You're all afraid of it. You have no idea about its whole trip, how it's sold . . . Do you know what 'cut' means?" He looked to a different person with each of these arguments. "Let me go. If Julien cheats you, all of this will have been for nothing."

"You speak no French," Nuria threw at him.

"So what. I know coke. I'll find Julien and give him a written message. No, better yet, you teach me what to say. Just the right words to get me started. When it gets to money, we'll understand each other."

The three Catalans reverted to their own language in their discussion. Brian wondered if they were talking about the one thing he had not mentioned: disappearing forever with their money after he'd sold the cocaine. But it occurred to him they would never consider that possibility—only real amateurs could be this trusting.

"It is agreeable," Santiago said to Brian. "You go to France. Now how do we conceal the cocaine for the frontier?"

The work on the motorcycle was soon finished, and Brian was at the Gerona crossroads at dawn, ready to take off for the border. He would have to drive carefully because there was cocaine instead of a brake cable running up the inside of the handlebars. Night driving was also out since the headlight wires had been gutted to allow for space to cram the rest of the kilo behind the reflector.

Brian revved the engine. He would find Paul in Paris after all this was over. It would be good to see his friend again once this coke business was off his mind. The quickest route to France was straight ahead on the Gerona road, but Brian inexplicably turned right, up the winding, slower coastal road. The decision made no sense if he wanted the treacherous border crossing to be over as soon as possible. But there was the strong attraction of the longer route which delayed the dangerous moment when he would know if he'd ever see Nuria again.

Dark clouds threatened rain, and the twenty thousand dollars' worth of cocaine at his fingertips made the coming storm even more menacing. *God, don't let it rain now!* He couldn't risk getting the cocaine wet, even though it was supposedly sealed watertight inside the skeleton of the motorcycle. Crazily, he accelerated through the dangerous curves, trying to lose the pursuing storm.

By the time he'd reached Gerona, the sky was clear. He shifted into a more comfortable position in his seat, trying to work out the kink at the base of his neck. Already there were aches, and he had only been in the saddle an hour. He was not in shape for long hauls after all those months in Tossa. The thought of all the remaining hours before reaching Paris made him hunch over; the kink returned.

Gerona was the first landmark of any importance on the map. The shake in the handlebars from the old cobblestoned streets was a pleasant diversion. From Gerona, it wasn't far to the next big town, Figueras. And from there, it was only a short sprint to the border. He could see the snow-capped Pyrenees in the distance, blocking his way into France.

The motorcycle shot down the home stretch, passing the lumbering diesel trucks to escape their black trail of exhaust. Nearing the row of border gates, Brian slowed down and fell into line behind a tractor trailer, for it was too late to pass it. The big trailer blocked his view as they inched forward between methodical stops after each vehicle cleared the gate. Brian wished he knew the procedure at the front of the line. A dry run would've made these anxious minutes a little easier to live with, but it was too late now. He rose off the seat to shake off his nervousness which, to everyone else, appeared to be a stretch to get rid of the stiffness.

The truck in front of him was now at the gate. He leaned sideways to see what was happening, but the trailer was too wide. Would it have been better to be a hitchhiker walking across the border with the cocaine? At least there would be less waiting: just stroll up to the gates and pass right through. Then Brian thought better of that idea, remembering an idle conversation in which someone had said that border guards thought all hitchhikers were dope-carrying hippies, and always searched them more zealously.

The gears of the truck engaged, and it pulled away. Brian opened the throttle gently to ease the motorcycle up to the gate. The guard in the booth was dressed in a brown uniform with red trim. He absentmindedly held out his hand for Brian's passport and routinely leafed through the pages.

Suddenly the lackadaisical mood of the guard vanished. He

scolded Brian in excited Spanish. Brian tried vainly to see which page the guard kept pointing to while he said, *"No hablo español,"* and shrugged his shoulders helplessly.

Now the guard was holding the passport over his head, signalling for help. Brian could see the row of black uniformed guards that marked the French border just a few agonizing yards away. It was torture to watch the traffic moving so easily through the other gates, with some of the drivers cautiously sneaking a glance in Brian's direction as they pulled away.

The guard pushed a button, motioning for Brian to remain there. The fear of a warrant for his arrest seized Brian. What was wrong? If they had wanted him they would have come to Tossa, he told himself. Don't panic. You're too close now. He looked over his shoulder, trying to appear unconcerned about the delay. Traffic was deserting his line for the other gates.

Another brown uniformed guard was finally coming over, taking what seemed forever to Brian to work his way across the other lanes of traffic. Upon arriving at the booth, the new guard tugged ceremoniously at his jacket and then examined the passport.

"When did you arrive in Spain?" the new guard asked in good English.

"Last February. I don't remember the date."

"Have you left since that time?"

"No, I've been touring."

"You work in Spain?" the guard inquired.

"No. I live on my own money."

Brian fought the temptation to follow the guard's scrutinous gaze. Was it his imagination, or were the guard's eyes fixed on the handlebars?

"You are in Spain nine months. It is necessary to have a visa for that much time."

Relieved, Brian sank down in his seat. "I didn't know."

"Where were you?"

"Mostly a place called Tossa."

"You have a good time?" the guard asked, as if he were following a routine dictated by the Board of Tourism.

"Great," Brian answered with equal indifference.

The guard in charge gave the passport to the other guard and then lectured with sincerity, "Next time you come to Spain, only six months."

The guard in the booth stamped *Salida* with the current date on the same page that read *Entrada* and included the date on which Brian had entered Spain. These two inconsequential marks comprised the entire official record of what had happened to him in Spain. Brian kicked the foot lever into gear. A few yards later, the black clad guard stamped him just as easily into France, beginning a whole new history.

He had entered France without a customs check. Could it be this easy? If so, he felt stupid for being so nervous. The little matter of overstaying his visa in Spain was stupid, too. More amateurism, this time on his part.

The road rolled on without buildings or turnoffs. He caught up with the lumbering truck that had been in front of him at the gate. Now that he was in France, the roar and exhaust of the truck only exasperated him more in his eagerness to reach Paris. He looked for a break in the oncoming traffic to pass, but the line of cars was endless. Coming around a long curve, he saw cars and trucks lined up at the side of the road. The sinking feeling from the Spanish side of the border returned. This was French customs! That's why there were no side roads. More amateurism on his part to have believed it would be so easy.

They were only randomly waving over cars. It was time to begin thinking intelligently. Brian pulled up close behind the truck in the hope that the customs guard wouldn't see him in time to pull him over. But the truck was waved over. It broke from Brian's line of sight, opening up the road ahead. He tried to appear unruffled by the black uniformed guard at the side of the road, and kept looking straight ahead. But out of the corner of his eye he saw the arm go up, waving him over too.

Brian knew customs was just a numbers game. The guards couldn't check everyone, so they chose the most likely bets. He cursed himself for not having cut his hair to reduce the odds. He would just have to stay cool. They weren't going to tear the motorcycle apart unless they had good reason, and he was clean, scrupulously clean.

The guard studied the rider and motorcycle as he leafed through the passport and vehicle registration papers. Brian tried to keep looking at the guard, but without staring at him directly in the eye. *It's the eyes. They spot you by the eyes. Eyes never lie. Stay straight and cool.* It was only necessary that the guard not notice the throttle cable running along the outside of the handlebars.

"How long will you be in France?" the guard asked in well-rehearsed English.

"A month, maybe."

"What do you have to declare?"

Brian pointed to the pack tied to the rear of the motorcycle. "Clothes, nothing else."

The guard took another look at the papers, as if he couldn't make up his mind whether he wanted to check further or not. "Is cold on the *motocyclette, non?*" he asked, flicking his eyebrows when he handed the papers back.

"Not bad," Brian yelled over the engine noise. He tucked the papers into his inside pocket, feeling the chill of the wind under his sweating arms. The guard stepped back and Brian slowly pulled away, giving the throttle a burst of speed to celebrate his victory.

The open fields of the border became the scattered beginnings of Perpignan, and then he saw the first road sign pointing to Paris. He made the turn and settled back in his seat, all set for the long, hard ride.

Things went so smoothly that Brian was in Paris by the early afternoon of the second day, feeling jubilant about the effortless journey. Mother Nature had cooperated, allowing no rain or snow. He would sell the cocaine and have the money on the way to Marseille by nightfall. He drove purposefully through the city, once again enjoying the thump of cobblestoned boulevards and the tireless energy of Paris, which was enthralling after the wintertime lethargy of Tossa. Every sidewalk was alive with people hurrying somewhere.

The cafe described in Santiago's directions had none of this frenzy, however. It was a grimy place on a corner of the Boulevard de Belleville, filled with a shabby-looking clientele in wrinkled clothes. Brian took a seat at one of the tables and ordered a coffee. The fact that the motorcycle was parked out of sight made him nervous, but there was nowhere nearby to leave it without the risk of it being towed away.

He sat enjoying his coffee. Having nothing to do but relax and wait for the first time since leaving Tossa was a welcome luxury. He was content to be as idle as the others in the cafe, watching the shops and open-air stalls along the center promenade of the busy Belleville.

After a time, the endless stream of humanity and honking traffic became depressing to Brian because he understood nothing going on around him. Here at his destination, spotting Julien from Santiago's meager description suddenly seemed an insurmountable task. For the first time since he'd decided to go to Paris, reality was settling in. He was in possession of twenty years' worth of prison in a country where he didn't speak the language, looking for a stranger who wasn't expecting him and whom he didn't know well enough to be sure he was telling the truth. What if Julien had said he was a dealer just to impress some girl he met on holiday? All these amateur antics they'd survived so far were not incredible, they were impossible.

Brian finished his coffee and scanned the cafe for the best person with whom to begin the search for Julien. He approached the woman at the cigarette booth. She sat at the register, too engrossed in her *Paris Match* to notice Brian at the counter.

"*Parlez-vous anglais?*" he asked buoyantly to get her attention.

She looked up from her magazine, replied, "*Non, Monsieur,*" and gave him a helpless smile.

"*Monsieur Julien ici?*" he said, trying to remember Nuria's instructions about softening the word endings in French.

The woman only shook her head, babbling on in French and pointing to the street. Julien's name was all Brian could decipher from her nasal outpourings, so he reciprocated smile after gracious smile while trying to unravel himself from her chatter, certain everyone in the cafe was watching. The bartender knew nothing either, but mercifully didn't go into a long-winded speech. He gave Brian only a curt shake of his head and politely waited for Brian to say something. There was nothing for Brian to do except order another coffee, which he carried back to his table.

A woman with blonde hair stiffly sprayed to hold the curls entered the cafe. She came toward Brian, unbuttoning her fur-collared gray coat before sitting down at the next table. Her silver high heels were obviously picked for the trim that matched the crimson color of her dress. A daydreaming look settled over her face after she ordered from the waiter, as if she knew the cafe too well to be concerned with its clientele.

Brian guessed her age to be somewhere in the late twenties. She wasn't beautiful or glamorous, but Brian felt drawn to the assurance of her bright face competently maintained with makeup.

When the waiter brought her coffee and cognac, Brian ordered a beer, not really in the mood to finish his coffee. When the waiter brought the beer, Brian asked, "You know *Monsieur* Julien?" All he got were more excited denials as the waiter backed away.

"Perhaps I could help," the blonde said in good English with the barest trace of an accent.

"You speak English?" Brian stammered, as if he couldn't believe his ears.

"Many people in Paris do," she answered with a glib laugh.

He studied her cautiously, really for the first time, wondering how her good looks would stand up to the truthful scrutiny of a sunny day on the beach without mascara or eye shadow.

"I'm looking for a man named Julien," he said, making up his mind to accept her help.

She summoned the waiter. They spoke in French for what seemed years to Brian. At one point in the conversation a small grin broke over her face, as if she knew everything, making Brian more impatient. What could take this long to say!

Her conversation with the waiter finally ended. She said, "Julien has not come here for a week. The police have inquired, also."

Brian's initial reaction to the mention of police was to drop the matter, but finding a translator was too good a stroke of luck to pass up. Against his better judgment he said, "Ask him if he knows someone who can find Julien for me."

The question, in French, seemed too short. The waiter stepped back with an emphatic shake of his head, looking in every direction but theirs as he beat a hasty retreat to the bar.

"He does not know," the blonde apologized. "I think he thinks you are police."

"Police! Do I look like police to you?" Brian made sure he was giving her his best grin.

"I know you are American and not police, from how you speak. These people are not sensitive to English. To them, you could be a Frenchman in the disguise of an American hippie! You could be . . . how do you say it, a policeman who is a spy?"

"You mean an undercover agent."

"Yes, that is it." She sat up straight while trying to catalogue the new word for future use. "If it is the Julien I think, he is the man they say sells dope."

"Perhaps I shouldn't bother to find him," Brian said lightly, hoping his faked levity didn't sound forced or unnatural. "A man I met in a restaurant in Toulouse said to ask for his friend Julien when I got here." She seemed indifferent to his quickly concocted story, but the explanation sounded so lame to him he wanted to change the subject. "I've never been to Paris before," he went on uncertainly.

"You will like it."

"May I buy you a drink for the favor you've done me?"

"No, thank you. I still have this one."

"Please, I'd be sitting here asking for Julien for hours, creating all kinds of suspicion if you hadn't helped me."

She relented and asked for another cognac.

After the waiter had left with her order, Brian asked, "Do you know Julien?"

"Only to see him. I do not buy from him."

"I'm sorry, I didn't mean it that way."

She forgave him with a pleasant smile.

"You speak very good English. Where did you learn it so well?"

"In school, but my English is good because I work in a—no, *an* American bank," she said, quite proud of her small grammatical victory. "I must speak it all day."

"What is your name?"

"Claude."

"Isn't that a man's name?"

"In French, many names are the same for men and women. In English, it is Claudia."

"May I call you Claudia? Claude makes me think of a man."

"If you like. What is your name?"

"Brian."

"That is a man's name," she said with approval.

"You live in this neighborhood?"

"Yes."

"I would not guess it to look at you." The remark puzzled her. "Your clothes. You are dressed very well, compared to everyone here—compared to me," he apologized, looking down at his own rumpled army jacket.

"I am dressed like this because I have just finished work."

The nervous waiter brought her cognac, staying as briefly as possible.

"What will you do in Paris?" she asked Brian.

"I don't know. Just kind of hang out, I suppose."

"I would like to leave Paris. I would like to travel to America."

"Paris seems much nicer to me."

"Not if you lived here all your life, as I have. For me, Paris is very boring. I go to work in the bank every day like a good *bourgeoise*."

"So why do you keep working in the bank?"

"The money is good because it is an American bank. My friends think I am wrong to wish to leave. I am the only one with my own apartment and can afford the *Cote d'Azur* in the summer."

"Is that what you really want?"

"I do not know. I dream of excitement in my life," she said, taking a cigarette from her purse.

"It's no different for Americans. They dream of coming to Paris," Brian said.

"I think you are from California," she said confidently as she lit the cigarette.

"Yes," he said, surprised by her accuracy.

"I can tell," she went on proudly. "California is an exciting place for me, with Hollywood and San Francisco. California, I think, is how you say 'action.'" Her accent thickened a little on the unfamiliar word.

"Just how you say 'action' makes it seem that way," he said.

After a moment of deliberation, as if she were trying to make up her mind about something, she asked, "What will you do now? Is it important you meet Julien?"

"No," he answered, trying to appear indifferent about Julien, but inwardly suspicious of her question. The thought that she could be a narc prompted a cold, discouraging look from Brian.

She felt the rebuff. It made her decide to leave. She put the pack of cigarettes in her purse and stood up from her half-finished cognac. "Thank you for the drink." Brian took her extended hand, holding it unconsciously a little longer than necessary. "Have a good time in Paris," she added politely before leaving the cafe.

With Claude gone, Brian was again conscious of being foreign and alone. He leaned back in his chair, angry about his foolish attack of paranoia that had driven her away. But all the talk about police made him certain it was best to proceed slowly. He would wait until the next shift of waiters and inquire again.

To kill time, he went for a walk. The boulevard was a bizarre mixture of small food shops and cheap furniture stores, each colorful and interesting enough to help pass the time quickly. After he grew tired of browsing, he checked the motorcycle, needlessly it turned out, for it remained untouched. He began checking the other cafes as possibilities for Julien's hangout. The indifferent shrugs he encountered at the mention of Julien's name convinced him the police had not been there; thus those cafes were probably not hangouts for the dealer.

Drained of ideas, he roamed the streets, watching people make their last-minute purchases before the shops closed. The outdoor market was folding up its tents. The sight of everyone heading for home made Brian homesick for Tossa. He went for another unnecessary check of the motorcycle, just to pass the time, and then returned to the cafe.

The same woman was in the cigarette booth, still absorbed in her magazine, but the waiter was different. Brian took the same table. The new waiter shook his head apologetically. He was certain he did not know Julien.

There was nothing else to do now but consider finding a place to stay. Travelling at night would be no problem since they drove in Paris without lights. Still, he didn't like risking the unnecessary exposure of having no front brakes or of leaving the motorcycle in the streets all night unguarded. He would just have to remove the cocaine from his bike and stash it with Paul or Dominique, the only people he knew in Paris well enough to trust. Feeling secure with that plan, he decided to spend the rest of the evening at the cafe in the slim hope of meeting Julien.

As the boulevard grew quieter and quieter in the passing hours, the cafe grew busier and busier, and Brian became more and more obsessed with each new male customer. He would study each for the slightest indication he was Julien, trying to eavesdrop on his conversation, or watching for someone to follow his suspect to the toilet, perhaps to complete a sale.

Brian brooded over the possibility that Julien might think he was a narc because of his questions and consequently split, or even the converse: that the waiters would tell the police about this suspicious tourist asking for Julien. And then the police would come with their own questions! They'd search his bike and find the cocaine. That grim thought made Brian push the papers for the motorcycle deep into the bottom of his pack. From now on he would say he'd hitchhiked from Spain.

The cafe clock crawled past ten o'clock. Prostitutes would come in from time to time and give him the nod, but as long as it had been since he'd slept with a woman, he wasn't up to it that night. He comforted himself with the promise to buy a French whore when this was over.

He started playing pinball out of desperate boredom, even though he hated the infernal machines. They always seemed to demand more delicacy than he had. Four quick games took all his change, so he was back at his table when he saw Claude enter the cafe. She had changed into a short-waisted denim jacket and matching jeans with a cheerful purple bandana adorning her neck.

"I saw you through the window," she said, coming up to his table.

"I'm still here," he shrugged guiltily.

"I was bored so I took a walk." The purple knot of the bandana against her throat had the provocative lure of a crown jewel on white satin. She sat down without waiting for an invitation, as if they were old friends. "You are still looking for Julien?"

"I've asked a bit," he conceded.

"That's why you've stayed here, isn't it?"

Brian grew rigid. He had diced with her long enough on this whole thing, but he would gamble cautiously in case she was a narc after all. "Yes, I'm looking for him. Someone told me I could make a score."

"A score? I do not understand."

"I could buy some dope from him."

"Oh, I see." She laughed cunningly, excited by the clandestine aspects of the transaction.

They talked until the waiters had placed all the chairs on the tables except theirs. "They are closing now," Claude said. "I am afraid Julien is not coming."

"It's not important." But looking at her face, he knew she didn't believe him.

"Would you like to come to my apartment for a coffee?" she offered with a modesty that both touched and intrigued him.

She led him down the narrow side street bordering the cafe, past shuttered shops and one last drab-looking bar still filled with people engrossed in card games. Brian saw they were approaching his motorcycle, now trapped dangerously close between two parked cars.

He circled the bike to make sure it had not been disturbed.

Noticing the tourist license from where she stood on the sidewalk, Claude asked, "It is yours?"

"Yes."

"One that big is very expensive in Paris."

"Will it be safe here?"

"Oh yes. Many people leave them on the street."

He walked back to her, but his eyes never left the motorcycle. "Perhaps we could leave it in your garage?"

She laughed. "This is Paris. Who has a car, much less a garage?"

The late hour and the deserted street only intensified Brian's apprehension. Suddenly, Claude's invitation wasn't as appealing as when they'd left the cafe.

She seemed to sense his change of heart. "My apartment is not far." She pointed to a doorway a few yards away.

She walked a few steps, but when Brian made no move to follow her, she turned to see what was wrong.

"All my money is tied up in this bike," he explained. "If anything should happen to it . . ."

"We could leave it in the vestibule with all the *bicyclettes*," she offered, trying not to sound unsympathetic.

Brian pushed the motorcycle to the street entrance of Claude's building. The doorway was one steep step up from the sidewalk.

"To turn on the engine will be too much noise," she warned when she too realized the obstacle he had been considering. "Can you push it in?"

"I think so, with your help," he said, deciding the momentum would carry the motorcycle over the step.

She held the door open. He ran the front wheel up and over the doorstep, but had to stop when he saw the engine block was not going to clear the edge.

"You'll have to steer while I lift the back wheel." He stepped away to let her take the handlebars.

As he bent to lift the rear end, Brian could see Claude awkwardly stretched across the gas tank with both hands on the handlebars, wriggling her hips in an unconsciously provocative little bump and grind to hold the front door open.

When Brian heaved the rear wheel up into the hallway, the unbraked motorcycle pitched forward without warning, catching Claude off guard.

"Brian, help me," she cried in a panicky voice. She had lost her grip on the handlebars.

Brian rushed forward, sandwiching her between him and the toppling motorcycle. He braced against the dead weight, at the same time sensing Claude's body squirming against him as they struggled together to keep the machine upright. For a moment it seemed they would lose the battle. But then Brian managed to balance the motorcycle and the previously unyielding weight was now evenly distributed, allowing him to set the kickstand in place.

"That wasn't too hard," he noted sarcastically while they both tried to catch their breath.

She straightened up in his arms, making no move to lessen the pressure of her hip pressing against him.

"That is my apartment," she whispered between short breaths, nodding toward a door just down the hall. "Perhaps your motorcycle would be safest in there. With us."

Brian never got his coffee. No sooner were they inside her apartment than he pulled Claude to the floor in a brutal flurry of rough kisses and torn buttons that left her naked except for the purple scarf still knotted around her neck like the collar of a tethered cat. She was frightened by his violence, but all this talk of dope and America had awakened a new person in her that did not cry out to stop the rape-like advances. She reveled in her newfound role of victim, fascinated all the more by the unknown danger. As he spread her coiled knees, she braced to accept him in silence.

They lay together on the floor, too exhausted to care about the stiff jute of the rug prickling their skin. Undressed, she was not as shapely as Brian had imagined in the cafe. A little thick through the hips and thighs, but only noticeably so when compared to the stiletto-thin Nuria. He pulled the blue afghan off the couch and wrapped it around them both. Claude's hair was matted and bristled from his clawing fingers. He gently stroked the ruffled strands straight. "It's crazy to lie here on the floor like this when there's a warm bed in there," he said.

"I like it," she mumbled child-like through the wide weave of the afghan, "And besides, we would disturb my husband."

"Your husband?" he started.

"Don't worry. He's blind and deaf. That's why he didn't hear us. I hate to make love with him. When he wants me, he ties me to the bed so I cannot escape."

Brian scowled until he heard her giggle at her joke. He kissed her affectionately, at the same time pulling them both up on their feet. Wrapped together in the afghan, they hobbled across the room and fell into the bed.

She started to untie the bandana. "No," he said, placing his finger on the knot. "Leave it. It makes you very sexy."

The light from the living room poured through the doorway. Slight lines in her face were already announcing the last years of youth. Brian sensed she would not live up to Paul's little tenet that French women age well. He kissed Claude to wash away the grievous thought, letting his hand slide along her inner thigh.

She caught hold of his wrist, stopping its advance. "No. I must work tomorrow. It is very late," she pleaded, but he kept kissing her until he felt her breathing quicken. And then she pulled him closer. This time he was completely consumed by his building orgasm which smashed to nothingness the pleasant memories of a summer beach town, the white nightmares of cocaine inside a motorcycle, and, in the paramount instant of pleasure, his love for a Catalan girl.

He could never sleep through the night the first time in a strange bed. He kept waking up in the darkness wondering where he was until he would feel Claude next to him. When he woke up and saw it was finally morning, he found he was alone. In the daylight he discovered the rest of the room beyond the bed. The walls were bare. No pictures, knickknacks, or anything you'd expect to find hanging in a woman's bedroom; not even a mirror. A bureau and chair hidden by the previous night's darkness stood along the opposite wall. They were the only other furnishings except for the wine crate that served as a nightstand on his side of the bed. He'd never known a woman to neglect her bedroom so much.

The shower going behind the closed door stopped. A minute later Claude came out of the steamy room wearing a yellow robe. Happiness came over her face when she saw he was awake.

"*Bon jour, mon animal.*" She sat on the edge of the bed nearest him. He nodded without a word, pretending to still be dulled by sleep. "What will you do today?" she asked, undaunted.

"I don't know." He began stroking the sleeve of her robe absentmindedly.

She swallowed before saying, "Will you be here when I come back from work?"

"If you like."

"I would like that." She leaned across his chest to kiss him. He pulled the seat of her robe up to her hips. "No. This time I must go to work," she scolded, breaking away to the dressing closet.

Modestly, she retreated deep inside the closet, to be out of sight before removing her robe. He slid across the bed to where he could still see her in the mirror hanging inside the closet door. The voyeuristic thrill of watching her, unaware of his eyes, dry herself with a bath towel and then slip into her underwear was causing another erection.

"Do you always keep men like this?" he called to her.

She came to the doorway of the closet. In only her slip and bare feet, the hurt look on her face gave her the frailty of a lost child.

"I didn't mean it that way," he said. "I'm not used to strange women taking me in like this. I'm not sure what I would've done without you last night."

She came over to the bed. "I don't know why I did it. I've never done it before . . . like this. These days I am very lonely and bored. I feel I have no value. I am twenty-eight years and I have had but one affair in my life. A married man from the bank. To him the affair was nothing more than the appropriate thing a man does at that time in his life. Like putting braces on his children's teeth. He stopped seeing me because that was appropriate too."

She took a cigarette from the nightstand but did not light it. "Now, my life is nothing. I feel I am asleep. You looked lost in the cafe and I sense you are exciting. You are an adventurer, no?"

"No, not really."

"You are. I know. What do you do?"

"What do you mean?"

"Your work."

"Nothing."

"*Oui.* You are what I said." Her gray eyes had become as delicate as filigree. "Give my life adventure," she implored from a pit of loneliness as deep as his own.

Even with the motorcycle nestled safely in Claude's apartment, the operation to extract the long white intestine from the handlebars still required the dexterity and patience of a surgeon to avoid rupturing the casing. Brian wondered how he could have done it in the street, where every unexpected sound threatened discovery by the police. Finally, he had the motorcycle back together and the packet safely in his pack. It was too late in the day to do anything else about Julien but give the corner cafe one more try.

On her way home Claude spotted him in the cafe. She approached unnoticed. "You are waiting for Julien?" she whispered indignantly over his shoulder.

The unexpected voice startled him. He turned. "This is not the place to talk about it," he said, trying to hold his voice down.

"You are an addict! That is it," she hissed. He could see it would do no good to talk, what with her state of panic building into hysteria. He tugged at her arm for her to follow him, but when she didn't move, he yanked harder. She let herself be led out of the cafe and back to her apartment.

Once inside her home, Claude began to cry. She sat riveted to her couch while he stood over her. After she seemed to have gained some control, he finally said, "I thought you wanted adventure. With adventure there's no questions, only acceptance."

"All day gives me time to think. I never think in the night. That is how I am involved with that man in the bank. Now I do not know."

"Do you want me to leave?"

"No." All spirit seemed to have gone out of her. "It is just you are so strange, *mon animal.*"

"This morning you said you wanted adventure. Ok!" He stalked into the bedroom, afraid he would regret later what he was about to do. He came back carefully holding the white coil in both hands like a dangerous snake and dropped it next to her on the couch.

"What is that," she screeched, just when she thought she had regained her composure.

"Cocaine."

His callous reply made her begin to crumble into hysteria again.

He overcame his own anger, speaking softly to choke off her panic. "Claudia, I'm no addict. I'm looking for Julien to sell this. Believe me, the money is for nothing bad."

"I believe you," she said, beginning to get a grip on herself.

He wasn't sure whether she really did believe him or just wanted to very badly.

"How much money do you want for that?" she asked.

"A hundred thousand francs."

"*C'est le pied,*" she whistled under her breath. The magnitude of the amount had a calming effect on her. All those years spent in a bank had instilled in Claude an unwavering faith in the rationality and stability of people who dealt with large sums of money.

Sensing the change in her mood, Brian thought it safe to pursue the idea he'd been considering all day. "Do you know any dope dealers?" he asked.

"No," she said. "Some of my friends use hashish, but I have never—"

"I'll have to find someone to help me sell it."

"That is very dangerous." Her concern for him seemed to calm her even more.

"I must find someone. I'll see my friend tomorrow. Maybe he can help me."

"Shall I come with you?"

"No, I don't want you to get involved . . . if I should get caught
. . . Look, I'll take the coke away tomorrow. It's not fair to you
that I keep it here."

"I will help you that much. This is the best place," she said,
picking up the long white snake gingerly, as if it were alive, and
carrying it to the bottom drawer of her dresser. She placed it
under her sweaters, making Brian chuckle at the obvious and
unimaginative hiding place.

"If I hide it too well," she reasoned, "you will not find it."

I don't think there has ever been a day that blew my mind as much as when Brian showed up at Christiane's door. I heard the knock and there was that uncanny grin waiting to be invited inside.

I couldn't believe what he told me. Cocaine! Killing a cop! Guns! Revolution! Jesus Christ!!!

When he'd finished, a kind of postoperative shock settled over me. All I could seem to do was grope dumbly for the pack of cigarettes under my chair.

Brian had plunged through, had grasped the true heart of Catalonia in those few short months while I, living in Tossa all those years, tripping along and balling every fox I could get in my sights, had remained oblivious to the real truth going on inside those people. I think it was Brian's desire to be involved that made the difference. He wanted to know about them. I envied him that white heat that somehow seemed to purify even such terrible things as guns and murder and cocaine to where they lost their sinister quality.

I was still reading it all in, stunned by the whole tale, and trying to digest each little episode when he asked, "Can you help me sell this coke, Paul? I need your help."

Sucking in a breath, I said, "I don't know," realizing how helpless I must've looked. "I don't really know the ropes here. Christ! How can I help you? I didn't even know what was really happening in Tossa."

Brian sagged back in the chair from the weight of his disappointment.

"You and Nuria." I shook my head in disbelief.

"Come on, it's not like that."

"It must be something unreal if you haven't balled her. What about this fox here?"

"Claude. She's nice . . . but I don't want to hurt her."

"How you not going to do that?" I persisted.

"I don't know. . . . Listen!" He gave me an angry look. "When'd you start worrying about hurting people? I thought you said everyone's got to handle their own shit. Just help me unload the coke."

"Brian, you know I'd do anything I could to help you, but there's nothing I can do here."

"What about Christiane?"

"She's out of town for a week. Man, neither you or me speaking French, trying to sell cocaine to strangers. . . . Why, that's insanity, man! Plain wild insanity!"

"Maybe . . . Dominique." He said her name hesitantly, as if he'd broken a personal vow not to drag her into this.

"She's not in Paris anymore. The airline transferred her to Nice. I have her address—"

"Never mind. . . . That's one I used up a long time ago."

Claude was in the apartment when Brian returned. "What are you doing home from work so early?" he asked.

"I worry about you. I cannot work, so I told them I was sick . . . and then you were not here." She looked down at her fidgety hands, embarrassed about her fear.

He kissed her on the forehead to show his appreciation for her concern. "My friend can't help."

"What will you do now?"

"Try to sell it on the street."

"That is for lunatics."

"That's just what Paul said."

"I have money to live," she argued.

"It's not for money for me that I do this. The money is for others."

"Why do they need the money?"

"You don't want to know, Claudia . . . and it's not important to you and me."

"I will help you," she stated confidently. "You cannot sell without speaking French. I ask my friends at work tomorrow."

"Claudia, I can't let you do this."

"I said I wanted adventure in my life, no?"

She was still dressed for the bank, looking formal in the herringbone skirt and matching jacket and with her hair pinned up. He smiled affectionately while undoing the blonde crown.

"Why do you laugh at me?" she asked defensively.

"I'm not laughing at you. I'm touched by what you're doing for me. Fate sends you when I'm desperate. You come into my life and help, asking nothing. You give so much and there's nothing I can give you."

"Brian, I want nothing. This time I live your *genre* of life."

In the past he would've emotionally run from her offering, but because there was meaning to his life now, he could hold her with love. Claude needed him, as he needed Nuria. He did not know which relationship gave a more lasting, stronger love, that is, if either could. The incompleteness of each one let Brian feel something good about both women without conflict. That was very important for Brian at this time; it meant he wasn't using Claude now, even though yesterday he had.

"What is the cocaine like?" she asked him.

"You want to try some?"

"No, it will make me an addict." She drew back fearfully.

"You can't become an addict from cocaine," he assured her,

remembering he had had the same fear his first time.

She said nothing.

"Trust me," he urged gently, and went for the packet of cocaine.

Claude sat on the sofa watching the long white packet curled up on the coffee table, while Brian rummaged through the apartment for what they would need. He laid the items out on the table in a straight line, as if they were surgical instruments for an operation: a mirror, a measuring spoon from the kitchen, and a razor blade.

Using the spoon, he scooped the shiny white flakes onto the mirror, and with the razor blade chopped the tiny pile into a fine powder. He then carefully drew the cocaine into four thin lines.

Claude gave him the newest bank note in her purse, which he rolled tightly with a folded corner tucked under to hold the cylindrical shape. With the homemade straw, Brian snorted one of the white lines up each nostril, and squeezing both nostrils with his fingers, he let go a "pop" of air.

"Now you try," he said between sniffles, and held the rolled-up bill out to her.

This dirty little ritual in which you stuffed foreign objects up your nose was not at all what she'd imagined. The snorting and sniffling were disgusting, so repulsive that she could not bring herself to reach for the straw.

What did she really know about this man offering the rolled-up bill, like the apple in a reverse version of Adam and Eve, tempting her into a world she had always been told to fear? If she accepted the straw she would be dropping into an unknown pit, which was very scary this close up.

Her apprehension changed Brian's small, inviting smile into a leer in her mind. He extended the straw further, but still she made no move to take it. She knew the decision came down to trust if she were not fooling herself about wanting adventure. There could only be newness if she would break the rules of her circumscribed world. She must have faith, not only in this stranger but in herself, if there were ever going to be change.

She took the bill from his fingers.

The unfamiliar motions made her feel awkward. She clumsily pointed the straw at the first line and inhaled, feeling the harsh burn in her nostrils as the cocaine disappeared up the straw. Exhaling a little too soon, she scattered the other line over the mirror like dandelion fluff. Brian gave her an understanding hug to ease her embarrassment. She moved the straw over the mirror, easily vacuuming up the remaining powder.

"I don't feel different," she said, leaning back on the couch, greatly relieved it was over.

"Give it time," he reassured her, leaning back next to her. He could already feel the pleasant numbness freezing his own front teeth. "In a few minutes you'll know."

The tense expression on Claude's face disappeared when she sensed the first rush. The surge in her body was not the harsh blows of some heart-pounding hammer, but a smooth acceleration in metabolic speed over which she felt control. She was ready for more, so he blew some of the cocaine into the back of her mouth. At first she grimaced at the bitter taste, but it faded quickly because of the numbing qualities of the drug.

The rush slowed. A steel band seemed wrapped tightly around the inside of her head. Her compressed brain was alert to everything within the reach of her senses, recording colors and sounds in the apartment she had never noticed before. Everything was brighter, louder, but in a delicate, soothing manner. She felt a compulsive need to share with Brian everything that was happening. Uncharacteristically, she chattered on, unable to stop talking except to catch her breath, deliciously cooled by her frozen nostrils.

Finally, she slumped back against the couch in exhausted silence. They snorted more lines, and Brian led her submissively to the bedroom. With her head thrown back, she lay on the cool sheets wearing only the bandana as his lips traced the slope of her throat with light kisses. She had never wanted anyone to make love to her so badly. Between her legs was a boiling cauldron that would rupture in orgasm at first touch.

He loosened the silk knot of the bandana. She could feel the kerchief being pulled away, making her free . . . free as smoke released by fire. She could not bear to wait for him, for anything any longer. She sprang up and pulled him down savagely, straddling him like a hungry cat over her surprised prey. Her thighs tightened like jaws, devouring his body in a glorious attack that seemed to pull her inside out until every nerve ending was on fire from the wall of light slicing through her hammering body.

Brian awoke. The drumming of raindrops on the bedroom window was the first sound he heard. The dreary daylight felt like morning, even though the alarm clock said three-ten. He looked again to make sure he'd read the time right, grunting smugly when the second hand did not move. He calculated it was Saturday. If that were true, they hadn't moved from Claude's apartment in four days. The thought of Claude made him reach for her beside him, but she wasn't there.

He called out her name.

"*Oui,*" was the distant voice from the kitchen. She brought him a cup of coffee and placed it on the nightstand next to the dead clock.

Since their first snort, the days had become a timeless blur of snorting and love-making right up until the nightmarish end yesterday. He had watched Claude's fascination with the rituals of cocaine grow until they were as much a part of the pleasure as the drug itself. She would spoon out the white chunks with great precision and care, chopping them up with an almost religious awe of their transformation into the magic powder. Best of all, she loved the inviting screech of the blade across the mirror when she combed the cocaine into regimental lines ready to do battle in her head.

It had been a wild time sniffing cocaine off knives, razor blades, belt buckles, fingernail files, whatever was handy, even the floor once when Brian spilled the packet. The day before, she had wanted him to tie her to the bed. While she struggled in her bonds, it occurred to him to pour a line of the cocaine down her spreadeagled body. He began to slowly snort his way down the smooth white skin. She tugged at the ropes, begging him to take her. He ignored the pleas, arousing her further until she thought she could not bear another teasing touch of the straw.

At last he was at the "V" of her thighs. He rubbed cocaine over both their genitals and made love to her in an endless climax that had her thrashing and screaming like a virgin on a sacrificial altar.

It was last night that the chameleon drug changed color, turning on Brian without warning. He craved cocaine, snorting every few minutes in a gobbling, futile frenzy to stay high. Finally he could not get high, even though he snorted more and more. His limbs grew heavy and trembled so much he had to concentrate just to hold the straw. His vision blurred. Everything seemed to be underwater. He lay in a cold sweat, unable to stop twitching. The jittery energy of the cocaine would not let his exhausted body sleep, nor do anything else—read, talk, or even make love to Claude, which he wanted more, in this perverse impotency, than anything else.

Brian took a sip of coffee. His stuffed nose felt like it had been rubbed raw with sandpaper.

"You are quiet," she said.

"Five days ago seems like a lifetime that never happened," he answered in a troubled tone.

"We have been happy, no?" She looked into his eyes for reassurance.

He cruelly rolled away, spying the packet of cocaine at the foot of the bed. Some had spilled on the floor. The little white mound could as easily have been Bromo Seltzer.

"We could go on like this forever. *Todo son flores*," he said, barely loud enough for her to hear. Suddenly he threw back the cover. "Come on, let's get out of here. Let's sell it before it fucks us up completely."

"Brian, can't we begin tomorrow," she pleaded.

He went into the bathroom to avoid facing that same temptation he too was having.

It was incredibly naive of them to set out in the rainy afternoon to find a drug dealer by simply walking around to the cafes, but they could think of nowhere else to begin. Claude would ask the bartender in French where they could buy dope, but soon after they began the routine, from each bartender's look Brian knew the answer without translation.

They did make one connection, but the dealer only laughed helplessly at the enormousness of the amount for sale. He didn't have that much money, and Brian had decided he would sell only the whole kilo. Anything less wasn't worth the risk and would still leave him looking for a buyer for the rest.

Sunday was fruitless too. They sat in the apartment fighting off the desire to snort away all memory of their failure. To escape the lure of the snakeskin in the dresser drawer, they went to a movie.

On Monday Claude went back to work while Brian spent the day at the corner cafe in a last, desperate hope to find Julien. He was cursing his luck when Claude rushed up to Brian's table. She had a name from a friend. Harry!

Harry could be found at a cafe near the Cluny stop on the Metro. They ran to catch the next train. By now they had been in too many cafes to take note of the expensive stainless steel fixtures or elegant copper bar that was Harry's address. They didn't even bother to order a drink, going instead right over to the table pointed out by the waiter where two black men sat talking.

"Harry?" Claude asked anxiously. The lighter skinned man looked up. He was small and skinny, boasting three chevrons on each sleeve of his imitation U.S. Army jacket. The other man, sensing the nature of the visit, immediately stood up to leave. That was a hopeful sign to Brian.

"You're American?" Brian asked, seeing the U.S. passport poking out of Harry's shirt pocket. More good luck than deserved, if he could do business with no language barrier.

Harry pointed to the passport. "You see. Yes, mon." The heavily accented English made Brian wary.

"Her friend . . ." Brian looked at Claude.

"Nadine," she said.

"Her friends say you deal."

Harry remained impassive. Brian gave him a few more seconds and then put his hand on Claude's elbow. "Come on. This is a waste of time."

"*Attends,*" Harry yelled after Brian's first step. "What you wish to buy, mon? Shit?"

"I'm looking to sell."

"What?" the dealer asked evenly. Brian had to admire the coolness. Not a trace of surprise showed in Harry's muskrat face.

"Cocaine," Brian murmured with effort.

Brian thought he caught a momentary flicker in Harry's eyes, but beyond that, the dealer continued to register more interest in the street than anything else. Harry finally said in a bored tone, "The quantity?"

"Almost a kilo."

"*Combien?*" Harry asked.

"He wants to know the price," Claude said.

"One hundred thousand francs."

"*Je n'ai pas bien compris,*" Harry said, as if he could not believe his ears.

"*Cent mille francs,*" Claude said.

Harry did not take his eyes off Brian. "*C'est du bon?*"

"He asks how good it is," Claude said.

"See for yourself," Brian said arrogantly, dropping a small folded piece of paper on the table. Harry gave a small jump of surprise before picking it up. Immediately, Brian felt foolish about the unprofessional act. This whole process was wearing him down and causing stupid mistakes.

Harry rose from the table, taking the small packet to the toilet. When he came back a few minutes later, he said to Claude, "*Si elle est toute comme celle-la, je l'achete.*"

"If it is all that good, he will buy it." Claude's voice rose, betraying her excitement.

It took everything Brian had to stay cool. "You have the money?"

Claude translated. *"Tu as l'argent?"*

Harry shook his head, going on in French. Brian's hopes were sinking again.

Claude said, "He does not have that much money now. He can have it tomorrow. He will telephone us where to meet him." She gave Brian's hand a tiny squeeze of delight.

"No," Brian said. "Tell him we'll call him."

"Non," was Harry's gruff reply, continuing in French.

Brian cut in, not letting him finish. "Claude, tell him we'll meet him here at noon tomorrow and if he has the money we will make the trade tomorrow night."

Claude started her translation. "And big bills," Brian added.

Harry listened, nodding every so often, obviously not happy with the arrangements.

At noon the next day Claude met Brian at the cafe. There was no sign of Harry. "Something to eat while we wait?" Brian asked, giving the place a careful look.

"Coffee is good."

"Let me buy you lunch. I've never bought you anything except a cognac that first day we met."

"No, I am too nervous to be hungry." She pushed her hands deep into the pockets of her red coat.

"It will be over soon," he said gently.

"I will be happy when it is finished. You are so calm."

"Not really. I'm scared too. In war you learn not to let it show."

Claude kept looking for Harry to appear at the entrance. Finally, she spotted him getting out of a taxi. Harry took his time, first stopping to buy a newspaper at the sidewalk kiosk, and then saying a few words to a passerby. He bought a drink before finally making his way to their table. He flashed a small, torturous smile to show he knew what he was doing.

"Il fait un temps splendide," he said.

"He says it's beautiful weather," she translated vacantly.

Brian only nodded. Harry went on, *"Je vais avoir l'argent."*

"He will have the money," Claude said, trying to hold to the lifeless drone of a translator.

"Tell him to meet us at the hotel at ten o'clock tonight, like I told you before," Brian instructed her. "No . . ." He touched Claude's arm to stop her before she could start. "Tell him eight o'clock. There's less chance of other guests in their rooms that early."

She recited the plan for Harry to meet them in the lobby of the Hotel de la Gare on the street next to the cafe. Harry said he knew the hotel. They left him with his drink and went out into the street.

"Well, it's done," Brian shouted over the traffic roaring down the wide St. Germain Boulevard. It was a beautiful November day, the sun as warm and soft as if it were spring.

They started walking hand in hand.

"What will you do now?" Brian asked.

"I go back to the bank, but I cannot do my work," she sighed.

They were standing at the corner where the Boulevard crosses the equally wide St. Michel.

"Come, you can show me the city. The worst is over."

"You cannot trust him," she said fearfully.

"Don't worry."

"You are good at that. I am not," she pouted.

He let go of her hand and turned her to him. He had to raise his voice above the crescendo of cars taking off from the traffic light. "You are the one who's good at this. You have everything to lose. I am brave because I have nothing."

"Then it is both of us who have nothing to lose." She looked down at the pavement.

He kissed her on the forehead. "My brave cat." In the furor of the busy street, his tenderness made her uneasy. She shifted her weight from one leg to the other. "We have the hotel room already," he said. "Let's go there now."

"I have to return to work," she said without much conviction.

"I've never made love in a hotel room in the middle of the afternoon. Have you?"

She only kept her eyes on the pavement, saying nothing until the roar of the traffic finally drove them away from the curb like the rush of a wave. And then she let him lead her down the small side street to the hotel.

The sand-crusted paths of the Tuilleries glittered in the late afternoon sun. They sat on the stone bench, enjoying the end of the day. Except for an occasional stroller, they had the garden to themselves.

Today for the first time since he'd arrived, Brian had enjoyed the special excitement of Paris. After making love in the hotel room, they'd walked along the Seine as the ponderous river barges floated past, and the *Arc de Triomphe* loomed up in the distance like the gates of heaven. They saw the busy commerce of the right bank, the hushed beauty of the Louvre, the splendor of Napoleon's tomb. These could have been the elements of any city. They were only monuments, museums, banks and department stores, but in Paris they took on a special glitter Brian couldn't explain. Perhaps it was the tranquil confidence of the old buildings, with their magnificent gargoyles and intricate facades aged to a peaceful gray over the centuries, that gave Paris this special aura.

The sun was sinking behind the Hotel des Invalides, changing the sky to a bruised purple. The lights in the buildings began to multiply across the silhouetted left bank. He could hear the tragic wail of a siren signalling sadness for someone.

"You are quiet," Claude said. "I do not like your silence today."

"It all goes on," he said, thinking how his own little drama, still to unfold, would be just another twitch lost forever in the roar and upheaval.

He turned to her. In the dying light he could see her face was tinged pink by the chill at the end of day. "You are cold and we must go back to the apartment anyway."

"Why?" she asked. "The cocaine is at the hotel."

"I want to get the motorcycle."

"The motorcycle. Why?"

"If there's trouble at the hotel, it will be faster to get away . . . and besides, I want to take you home before I go back there."

"I will not be with you at the hotel?"

"No, it's too dangerous."

"He doesn't speak good English."

"We'll make ourselves understood." He turned from her, pretending interest in the traffic to make it seem he was sure of what he'd said.

"I will come," she said firmly. "A misunderstanding is more dangerous."

"I can't let you do it, Claudia." The rays of the vespertine light painted her face in soft hues, making her more beautiful to him than ever before.

"It is final that I go. I have been in this with you all the time and I will not stop now." She stood up ready to leave for the apartment. "It is finished."

"If anything goes wrong, you could go to jail . . . you could get hurt."

"Brian, without you, without this adventure, I have nothing. You have given me excitement . . ." She held out her hand to him, still sitting on the stone bench. "The love. Come, we go to get your motorcycle."

"You do more for me than I have any right to ask."

"I think women always are that way with you."

When he stood up he could see the resignation in her eyes of someone who believes she is imprisoned by fate.

The *Arc de Triomphe* looked soft and hopeful in its golden spotlights, making Brian feel secure for the moment. She slipped her arm through his, and they strolled along the path like lovers on a casual promenade. He turned to catch the last glimpse of her beauty as it was captured by the sunset. She was biting her lower lip fearfully.

I don't know if it was curiosity or nostalgia about the Hotel de la Gare that made me arrive early. The old cockroach pit had been my first home in Europe after leaving the States. Except for the magazines, the lobby was exactly the same as before, right down to the two threadbare armchairs flanking the radiator. Seeing the old place was like looking through the family scrapbook— enjoyable if you don't do it for too long a time.

I was seated in my favorite chair reading a magazine when Brian came downstairs with the grim-faced girl who I gathered was Claude. Her red coat and blonde hair were the only cheerful things about her. If she'd had some color in her face (she couldn't have been that pale, even without makeup), I'd have called her attractive, but not slender and foxy, the way I like the French.

Brian acted like we were strangers, so I stayed in my chair playing tourist as he'd instructed on the phone that afternoon. They went to the front door and Claude said something in French to this black dude in an army jacket who was the "Harry" Brian had mentioned. I listened to the three of them climb the creaking stairs.

The room Brian had rented was drearier than the lobby, having only a small wooden table and chair and a cheap cotton mattress that sagged in the shape of someone sleeping. The ceiling was the roof of the hotel, sloping to the front wall so that you could not stand up straight except in the center of the room. Everything and everyone looked cold and menacing in the harsh glare of the one bare light bulb that hung from the ceiling.

"Ask him if he has the money!" Brian ordered, a little too sharply.

Harry came up with his roll of thousand franc notes before Claude said a word. Brian impetuously reached for the bread, but Harry pulled back, jabbering in French.

"He wishes to see the cocaine first," Claude said.

Brian brought the long white bag out from under the mattress. The two swapped goods guardedly, still instinctively fearful of the possibility the other was a narc. Harry dragged the small table away from the wall, to stand behind it and cover his blind side. Brian couldn't keep his mind on counting the money. There was still danger because if Harry was a narc, he'd be sure the dope was real before making the bust.

Harry weighed the coke with a small scale and then said something which made Claude say, "He says it is not a whole kilo."

Brian didn't look up from his money count. "Tell him it's close enough for that price and quality."

Harry grumbled in French without waiting for the translation, mostly, I think, for effect. He took a test sniff.

Brian finished his count. "It's all here. Ask him if he's satisfied," he told Claude.

Harry wasn't happy yet. While he was waiting for the drug to take effect, he did some other tests, including one where he took out a small square of aluminum foil to cook a spoonful over his gas lighter. The sight of the telltale reddish-brown flame made him happy. He muttered in his thick accent, "Good freeze, mon. It is *la cocaïne.*"

"That's it," Brian crowed, hardly believing it was finally over and he could relax.

In that instant he made just the kind of mistake his animal wariness had not allowed up to now. Harry, sauntering slowly from behind the table as he put the dope in his pocket, got Claude between the two of them. Suddenly, Harry's motions sped up. Brian realized too late what was happening. Harry caught Claude around the waist and simultaneously his hand came out of his pocket with the precise click of a switchblade. Harry held the point of the knife under Claude's chin, hissing orders in French.

Claude was so scared she could barely get the words out. "He says to give him the money."

Harry was really digging this, too. He was jabbing the knife upward to make Claude stretch in little bounces to stay off the blade, while at the same time grabbing a quick feel with his free hand.

"You bastard!" Brian cried, holding out the money.

Harry took back his roll and then pushed Claude forward, still holding out the knife.

Claude stood frozen between them. "I am sorry, Brian. It is my fault," she sobbed.

"Move away, Claudia . . . move away," Brian begged.

She didn't move. She didn't seem to hear him. "Brian, we cannot let him go with the money," she said, turning toward Harry's knife.

"Claude, for God's sake, come behind me . . . please." Brian reached out for her. That made Harry instinctively parry the knife, so Brian pulled his arm back, saying, "Claude . . . trust me." She finally began to take steps toward the window.

Harry extended the knife, edging backwards to the door. He blindly found the latch and backed out of the room right into my arms where I was waiting for him. "Bastard!" had been our signal. I caught Harry from behind, pinning his arms to his side.

I still don't know what I was doing there. There was no percentage for me in this. Only risk. I had to be crazy, but I couldn't let Brian try and pull this off by himself after he'd told me everything. There were too many ways it could go wrong.

Harry was so small and surprised it was easy to push the little weasel back into the room without too much fuss. Brian grabbed the knife out of his pinned hand. Brian's own hands were shaking so much with rage when he pulled the money out of Harry's pocket that some of the bills dropped on the floor. Harry wasn't in good shape, either. When I let him go, his knees sagged, making him look like he was hanging from an invisible hook in the ceiling. He wouldn't even move his eyes to follow Brian circling him as he picked up the spilled money.

I want to think Brian put his hands on the back of the chair to steady his nerves and nothing else. That what followed was just an impulsive explosion. I was thinking, "What now?" and looking around the dreary room when Brian screamed, "You God damn motherfucker!"

I turned just in time to see the chair come crashing down on Harry, who crumpled like a man who'd stepped in front of a moving bus. The blow from the chair pitched him all the way across the room, where he fell at the foot of the bed. Poor Harry. I could have felt sorry for the miserable son of a bitch if he hadn't brought it on himself.

I'd never seen Brian like that before. Nothing had mattered that much, even though he'd wanted it to. All this had given him something, after all.

"Claude," Brian said, patiently regaining his composure to where his fury only showed in his clenched fists. "Ask him if he has any friends waiting. Tell him it better be the truth or I'll carve the son of a bitch into little pieces with his own knife and feed him to the pigeons."

Claude asked poor Harry, who was still on all fours and shaking like a kid waiting at the whorehouse for his first piece. Harry had no voice. He could barely manage to shake his head for "No." He just kept his eyes glued on the money and dope laying on the bed. All those goodies so close and yet so far away!

"Claude, go down to the motorcycle. I'll look from the window to make sure you're ok," Brian ordered.

"I stay with you," she said. I was glad she'd suggested it because I was going to if she hadn't.

"Go down!" Brian growled, moving on Harry.

"Brian, take it slow," I said. "I don't give a damn about this prick, but they got your passport number on the register. We don't want trouble."

"I'm all right." He waved me away and again motioned for Claude to leave. She looked to me, not knowing what to do.

"Go on," I said with little pleasure. "We'll see this out Brian's way."

Brian went to the window to watch for her while I kept an eye on Harry. For Harry the minute it took Claude to reach the street had to be forever. From his terrified gaze, there was no doubt he was wondering what would happen to him.

But he also faced the added horror that he couldn't even beg or buy his life back without Claude there to translate. That must've been the final unnerving fear, for he started going on in little whimpers that were more and more uncontrollable as he tried to hold them back. Which only made the little bucking spasms worse and worse until he was shaking so bad I just wanted out of this whole ugly scene.

Brian saw Claude appear in the street. He came back to Harry. "God damn you," he cried, stomping his foot on Harry's hand so suddenly it gave me a start. Harry was so paralyzed with fear that no sound came out after the blow. Not a yelp, not a squeal of pain, nothing but the tiniest break in the rhythm of his sobbing.

"You won't be using knives for a while now," Brian added coldly as he walked around Harry to get to the other hand.

I grabbed Brian. "Cool your act!" I yelled.

Brian broke free of my grip. I thought he was going to stomp Harry's other hand. "You're getting freaked, Brian. God damn it! This ain't Viet Nam!" I shouted. The words jerked Brian away like the flat edge of a hot blade pressed against his balls. We were nothing but tired and dying men in the long shadows of the lone light bulb.

"We can't kill the animal in us, can we, Paul?" Brian said after a time in a shaky voice. "I wanted to kill him," he went on in self-amazement.

He reached down to Harry, who jumped a foot at the touch. Finally Harry let us help him to sit on the bed. We sat with him for a while as he tried to pull himself together. Every so often an uncontrollable sob would gurgle out of his throat, but he still couldn't say anything.

"You should get nothing for trying to rip us off, but I guess we've all paid our dues here," Brian said, taking only the money and leaving the cocaine on the bed.

Even that didn't make Harry look any better, but there was nothing else for us to do but leave.

When we got down to the street, the city still lived on. People were buying newspapers and warm crepes at the sidewalk stands or waiting in line for the movie. Every so often one of us would look back over our shoulder as we stood on the curb while Brian told me what had happened in the room before Harry backed into my arms. I guess we were looking for Harry to be walking up the street out of our life, but Harry never showed. He could've left the hotel and gone the other way, but somehow I don't think so. I'm sure he stayed in that room all night with the light on, doing coke and trying to get himself back to where it was good and sweet.

Paul—
Sorry I missed you. Gone shopping for a suitcase to put the money in, and then to the train station to check it through to Marseille. I'll stop by if there's time after that. I'm determined to make Tossa in two days so can't hang around too long. Thanks seems too inadequate for what you did to help me. I had no right to ask it of anyone, not even a good friend like you. If I don't come back after the train station I'll look for you after it's all over . . . or some summer again in Tossa.
Always, amigo,
B.

After I found the note pinned to the door, I waited around the apartment all afternoon, but the only knock on the door was Chris trying to surprise me. She'd come home from her trip a day early. Her smile soured when she saw I was disappointed she was not Brian. She pouted the rest of the afternoon because I wasn't paying much attention to her after she'd gone to all this trouble to rush home. I can't really blame her for being angry, but I could think of nothing else except Brian.

He never came back that afternoon, and Chris and I slid from sullen silence to childish squabbling. I couldn't stand it in the apartment any more, so I went for a walk by myself.

Whatever possessed me to go over to Claude's I'll never know. Maybe it was the faint hope Brian would be there, but down deep I knew better. Still, being with Claude just then seemed the right thing. I sensed something about her that made me certain she would understand what I was going through. I was going to see her like you would see family to share the grief over the loss of a loved one.

She answered the door in a bright yellow bathrobe that subdued the blonde color of her hair. She stared vacantly through the crack of the open door. Then she recognized me. "Hello," she said uncertainly, still making no move to open the door further.

For a moment I regretted coming at all, but it was too late for that. "I felt like company tonight . . . may I come in?" I asked.

She undid the safety bolt and let me in. The apartment was old with high ceilinged rooms. I commented how nice it was, which made her feel obligated to show me around.

We took seats on the couch in her living room as far from each other as possible.

The couch was terrible. It made you sit up straight, making me feel even more intruding and regretful about this surprise visit.

"Brian is gone?" I asked.

"He left this morning," she said.

After a moment I said, "I would've called first but Brian only gave me your address."

"It is ok. He said you live with a girl in Paris."

"That's right. She came back from a trip today but it just didn't feel right. I guess I wasn't ready for her after last night."

"I feel the same. Today, I could not stand people, either. I had a stupid fight with my best friend at lunch." Claude gazed at her lifeless hands resting in her lap. "Would you like a drink? I have some wine."

She went to the kitchen for the bottle. "Did you see Brian today?" she called.

"No," I said, unconsciously standing up and going toward her voice.

We met in the hall. When she handed me the glass of wine, her robe unintentionally flared open. She had seemed the nightgown type to me, but she was wearing nothing under the robe. Usually a glimpse of cleavage like that is more than enough reason for me to make a run at a fox, but that night even such an enticing act had no effect. There wasn't even the slightest glint in my eye when she blushed apologetically about her accidental tease.

The awkward moment sent us back to the couch where I discovered a purple scarf wedged between the cushions. When I handed it to her, she gave a furtive smile and for the moment was lost in her own reverie. Suddenly, she remembered I was still there, and folding the scarf neatly, put it in the pocket of her robe.

"You know Brian long?" she asked.

"Not really. Only since the spring."

Looking at her and the world she lived in, I felt we hadn't shared the same Brian, except for last night. She seemed to sense this also, for Brian dropped out of the conversation—that is to say we talked around him, about the rest of our lives: Paris and Tossa, her job at the bank, my bar, other things like that. I was counting the minutes until I could leave gracefully. Finally all conversation was exhausted.

We sat silent until she burst out, "I am glad you came tonight. It means Brian was here. It was not a dream."

Her words made me realize we were in the same world after all.

"Do you know what the money is for?" she asked.

"No," I lied, wanting to respect Brian's reasons, whatever they were, for not telling her.

"He would not tell me, even last night when he was leaving. He said he didn't want me to know him that way." She was pensive for a moment and when I said nothing, went on. "To help without reasons gives our time together something no one can ever have with me. It will always have its own unique character. I am glad you do not know, Paul."

It had begun to rain hard. The storm recalled the night before for Claude. She began to tell me how she and Brian had just arrived home when the rain started. Brian had been euphoric. He had said how lucky he was about everything all of a sudden; even the rain had waited until they were home.

Later, when they were in bed he'd slipped away to the window to watch the night. She'd said nothing, but he'd sensed she was awake. He said, "I keep telling myself I should not go back, but I have to, Claudia."

Claude watched him take the money out of his jacket and count off 5,000 francs. He put the bills on the nightstand saying, "This is for you."

"You are leaving." The moment she'd been dreading since they met had finally arrived.

He sat down on the bed. "In the morning I must go."

"Why?"

"Claude . . ." He could think of nothing that would make it any easier.

"Money! I don't want the money!" she cried, sweeping the bills off the nightstand onto the floor. "The money is not important. I did it for you and for what you give me."

"I've given you nothing."

"Nothing. There is nothing between us?" She was plainly wounded at the very idea.

"You know that's not true. I want us together, but it's really no good. I'm no good. Don't you see I'm an emotional hustler? I've always gone where it's best. A better thing comes along and I'm gone."

"There is someone else," she reasoned.

"A girl in Tossa," he conceded.

"A girl you love?"

"Yes, but in a different way than I love you. That's why I must go back. I must see it all the way through. The coke is only part of it."

"And me? What am I to do?"

"Wander. You see me as adventure and I'm not. That's finished in me and you still have to do it. That's why I want you to have the money, Claudia. Spend it on adventure."

"Without you it is no good."

"You only think that now. You've got to live it yourself, not through me."

"You are returning to Spain?" she asked bitterly.

"I've got to finish what I've started. It's very important to me because I've never done that before. If I hadn't met you in the cafe, I may have quit the whole thing like everything else in my life. You've given me the strength to finish . . . and now you're the temptation to quit."

"I understand nothing . . . except you are leaving, *mon animal*," she said, I imagine, in a long sigh like the one she let out while telling all this to me.

We had unconsciously moved together on the couch to the point where I could've put my arm around her if I wanted to. She hadn't meant this closeness to be an invitation for balling. It was only her way of asking me to help her understand. But I sat mute, feeling castrated in a way more terrible than sexual. How really useless I was in this world. I could not help Claude or anyone for that matter—not even myself. All I knew how to do with her or any fox was ball. A stud good for nothing else.

Suddenly I stood up, giving some lame excuse about having to leave because of another appointment. I ran from Claude like I'd run from everything else in my life; trying to convince myself I'd left because the whole lousy business with Brian and her was finished. So why stay or worry about it any longer?

It was lousy with Chris that night. She demanded to know where I'd been, which made it easier for me to torment her in revenge for my own inadequacy. God! I felt so old. I kept arguing how could she understand what I really wanted that night when she only had balling on her mind? She lapsed from anger into distraction and confusion and then began to cry. I had no defense against that. I didn't know what else to do except take her to bed.

It was horrible together. I couldn't make it with her and this only hurt her more. She wanted so much to be wanted that night. We were like two cripples together, unable to help each other.

I couldn't sleep. All I wanted to do was split. Munich! Stockholm! Amsterdam! Anywhere the next plane out of Orly went was ok with me. It turned out to be London, and as I watched the murky channel below, so cold and unforgiving in the morning light, I was trying hard not to care about anything.

Those days in the "bed and breakfast" near Paddington were the same to the point of being numberless. I don't even know how long I was there. I didn't phone Pete or Terry or any of my English friends from all those Tossa summers. All I did was sleep all day and then go out to a different pub each night and get good and loaded and try to nail the dumbest, most boring fox I could find.

Brian was retracing his route through Gerona for the fourth time when he finally spotted the "Tossa de Mar 39" sign behind the branches of an overgrown bush. Since he'd entered Spain he'd been driving on pure instinct. He looked at his watch, though he knew it would remind him how tired he was. Two o'clock in the morning. No wonder he'd missed that sign so many times. Only thirty-nine kilometers to go. He could still reach the Llibertat before it closed.

He knew the road to Llagostera well from the times he'd driven to Gerona on errands. From here to the hills was a straight run, probably with no traffic at such a late hour. He opened the throttle. New waves of refreshing cold air brought him back to life. Somehow, riding on that dark road at one hundred and twenty kilometers per hour wasn't at all dangerous.

He was riding to tell Nuria she'd have the guns. He'd given her the guns. It was all over. Why did he have to arrive and begin the end? One hundred and thirty kilometers per hour. One thirty-five. One hundred and thirty-five kilometers of madness! He knew the road. It was all over. If it could only be like this forever. Riding in the dark, your whole world held in the beam of an onrushing headlight. Always arriving.

He was too cold and tired at this point to be tense. Nuria. Claude. Nuria. Claude. Claude. What the hell had gotten into him, offering payment for services as if she were some whore he'd picked up on the streets? Why couldn't he have loved Claude enough not to leave her? Why did he have to love Nuria so much he would leave her? He could fight for her guns, but not Catalonia. It was her Catalonia, not his.

He'd given her the guns. One hundred and forty kilometers per hour. Oh yes, to always be arriving!

After the turn at Llagostera the road was still straight, but Brian slowed down, sensing the approaching hills. A slight uphill climb signalled that the last lap of his journey had begun. In the encapsulated world of the headlight, each curve of the twisting road became indistinguishable from the next. Soon a rhythm settled into his driving: accelerate up the grade, brake at the apex, power through the curve. On to the next turn. Accelerate up the grade . . .

Why was he coming back? He could have met them in Marseille. Or just sent word how to find the suitcase. No, it had to be like this. Going back to Tossa was the only way he could be sure.

Maybe he'd go back to the States after Tossa. Maybe he could . . .

Accelerate up the grade . . . Jesus Christ! Whoa!

The hairpin turn appeared too soon, its dirt shoulder quickly eating up his little world of illuminated asphalt. His body was straightening up even before he gave the command. Arms and legs stiffened in a hard brake, the reined-in motorcycle fishtailing from side to side like a bucking bronco trying to throw its rider. Miraculously, the motorcycle chose to slide in the direction of the arc of the curve, granting Brian enough smooth pavement to regain control of the skid. He dropped both feet for balance and extra drag as the motorcycle slowed, and came to a stop with the front wheel in the dirt. The headlight lit up a deep gulch directly in front of him, not three feet away.

He made no move to leave right away. The engine idled innocently, obediently awaiting his next command. He looked at his right hand still tightly wrapped around the useless front brake lever. If it had worked, the front wheel would've locked in an uncontrollable skid and sent him over the edge.

Finally, he felt steady enough to lift one foot off the ground. He slowly wheeled the motorcycle around, taking one last look at the blackness now hiding the gulch which had looked deep enough to keep his mangled remains a secret for years. Nuria would've continued to run the Llibertat. And Santiago and Marcello would have gone out in the boats each night. One day they all might even have gotten married. Have children! Brian began to laugh mockingly at himself as he drove up the hill, watching for the next curve in the headlight. Yes, how nice to always be arriving!

By the time he'd reached the Gerona crossroads he was tired enough to be tempted to go directly to La Vida and bed. At the bottom of the hill leading to the Llibertat the exhaustion from two very long days over the handlebars was replaced by a drained feeling of satisfaction. He parked the motorcycle and walked up the hill to surprise Nuria.

The swollen door quivered before opening. Exhaustion flooded back into Brian's body at the sight of the empty bar. *Where was Nuria?* He felt a rush of panic. *The police had come while he was gone!* Then he saw her in the archway leading to the back room. She ran to him and *she* kissed *him* for the first time. The kiss caught him off guard. It was the one fantasy of this reunion he hadn't considered during the long ride.

For the first time he did not feel an outsider in the Llibertat.

"We were afraid for you. You are at Paris so much days," she said.

He followed her through the archway to the fireplace. Marcello and Santiago were seated by the fire. They tried to share Nuria's happiness at his safe arrival, but the anxiety on their faces about the cocaine was obvious.

"We stay here each night for you," Nuria went on nervously.

"All is well?" Santiago interrupted with the unfeeling tone of a general more interested in a report on the mission than his soldier.

Brian handed him the railway claim check, saying, "I couldn't find Julien but it's done. There's a green suitcase in the train station in Marseille checked under that ticket. It has some clothes . . . and one hundred thousand francs."

Santiago extended the ticket so the others could see the prize.

Their admiring gaze made Brian self-conscious about his success. "I was lucky. This girl found someone."

Brian searched his pockets and then produced a key. "You'll need this too, to open the case. I bought the strongest one I could find."

Santiago put the key and ticket in his pocket. "We depart for Marseille tomorrow."

"Tomorrow is soon," Nuria pleaded. "We stay in Tossa some days."

"Why?" Santiago asked.

"Brian returns and I leave. It no is good."

Santiago started up in a flurry of Catalan before catching himself and changing to English. "If we wait, perhaps they sell the guns to others. Already we are late. You will be with Brian when we return with the guns."

"No! It will be different for all of us when the guns are here. You and Marcello go and I signal from the cliff. Brian does this because he loves me. I no can leave him so soon. After the guns, *¿quién sabe?*"

"Nuria, we cannot go to Marseille without you. You are the one who speaks French."

"No—"

"Nuria, we dream for years . . ." The begging eyes killed all meanness in Santiago's unshaven face. "You do not remember what we dream as children. Please do not lose this for me when I am very close."

Nuria looked away to Marcello's bewildered face. The words made little sense with his poor English, but he understood enough to return her worried look.

"Nuria," Santiago kept on, "the whole plan is this way because you speak French. Everything is complete. Only you can do this part in Marseille." Santiago paused and then spat out with contempt, "Brian has done more for your *Catalunya* than you."

The taunt made her glare. "Enough! We go," she said grudgingly and looked at Brian. "There is time for us when I return with the guns," she explained, asking for his reassurance with her eyes.

"*Molt bé*," Santiago said, knowing it was best to close the subject. He assumed the role of commander again. "Nuria and I take the Gerona train tomorrow afternoon. Marcello will be at the cliff to help us in. It is finished," he concluded, looking around at each of them.

Nuria locked the door after her cousins left and came back, bringing Brian a whisky. "For the cold in you," she said, handing him the glass. "No more peoples will come tonight. I close the bar."

He took a sip and waited for the first warming flush of the alcohol. It was his first chance to look around the room since arriving. It had not changed; only he had changed.

"I am sorry we will not be together before the guns," she said.

"I understand."

"I do not," she cried angrily.

"Nuria, don't you see? It always had to be this way. Don't you weaken now."

She held silent.

"Your father would've gone to Marseille tomorrow," he said.

"My father in me . . ." The words came out of her sourly. "It is poison. It kills my mother for me. Now it kills you, too. I hate the blood of my father in me tonight."

"You don't mean that. It is only more love I have for you because you do this when it would be so easy not to."

"You no can love the one who will kill. That is why you tell me to go."

"I love the one who gives up so much. You teach me the measure of love is sacrifice."

She took a sip from the drink in his hand to somehow join them together. He finished the rest of the whisky and she went to refill the glass.

"Paris was difficult?" she asked, setting down the fresh drink.

"Yes, but luck and Paul helped me."

"Paul knows?" she asked in shocked concern.

"Only about the guns and the cocaine."

"I never think Paul is the man to help a person," she said.

"He does it for me like I do it for you."

"Before he no was important to me. Now I am sorry I never see him again."

"I don't think Tossa will ever be the same for him after this," Brian said with a wry smile. "It won't be the same for any of us."

Nuria fidgeted with the glass, as if she were trying to make up her mind about something. "The girl who helps you is Dominique?" she asked in a low voice.

"No. She's someone I met and did much for us because of me."

"She is good. You love her."

"In a way. It's not the kind of love that should hurt you, Nuria."

"Perhaps it is better if you go to her."

"You are so beautiful to me. Tonight you would risk everything to be with me, even when I see the uncertainty in your face at the mention of her. She can't take your place. She is a different part of my life."

"She sleeps with you?"

"Yes."

"I no can sleep with you, Brian. I am glad she did."

Brian's involuntary shiver caused Nuria to stir, but not awaken. Uninhabited so long, Paul's living room was no warmer than their cave. Brian was the one bone tired, and she'd dozed off while they sat talking on the sofa. She'd insisted on walking him to La Vida even though she could not stay long because Madeleine might wake up and miss her.

He would let Nuria sleep. What did it matter now if Madeleine worried? Nuria was leaving her tomorrow. And Brian too in a few days, now that their plans had changed.

Brian would travel to Marseille with them. The thought had occurred to him as they walked to La Vida. At first it was agreed to part when the train arrived. Then he decided to wait until they had the guns. Three people were better than two if something should go wrong.

Now that he'd insisted on helping to buy the guns, he understood better than ever why Claude had come to the hotel that night. He was glad she'd been so stubborn. Refusing the money saved him from the final shame of having to live down such a callous gesture.

What did he have to do tomorrow—his last day in Tossa? The motorcycle! The hell with it. Paul could sell it and send him the money.

Brian stretched his cramped leg out, careful not to disturb Nuria. So what was wrong? This was the happiest moment of his life, and yet he didn't feel good about it. Nuria was so excited about the train ride now that he was going. With luck, she said, they would have a compartment all to themselves. She'd promised to chase Santiago away so they could be alone all the way to Marseille. So why could Brian only fake a similar joy at the prospect of their journey together? He'd been the one who couldn't bear to sit around Tossa and wait for her like some sidelines spectator while she smuggled guns into Spain.

Suddenly he realized he couldn't go to Marseille, either. It would be just as lousy as waiting around Tossa. He'd just spend all the time they were together counting the hours left. Even the jungle was not that cruel. It never told you when.

He couldn't go with her. He couldn't stay behind. But he couldn't leave, either, without knowing what happened to the guns. No, it wasn't finished yet. That was what was troubling him. It just wasn't over.

He prodded Nuria. She sat up and rubbed her eyes like a little girl. "I'm sorry. I was the one who wanted to talk."

At first he didn't answer. He was waiting until she was fully awake. "I have a change of plans for tomorrow."

"There!" Santiago yelled into Brian's ear after the motorcycle had cleared the tunnel cutting through the hill. Brian looked where Santiago was pointing; it was the housing development in the ravine below. He turned off the coastal road onto the service road of the apartment complex and wound down the hillside, stopping where the road ended at the cliff overlooking the blue Mediterranean.

Brian killed the engine and followed Santiago over to the final lamp post at the edge of the cliff.

"This is our way to find you. I hope it works." Santiago squinted hard at the light bulb, looking for some nonexistent sign that it would be on at night.

"Why shouldn't it work?" Brian asked.

"In Spain you cannot be sure anything works—the electricity, the water, the *butano*. Brian, you are here long time enough to understand that." Santiago grinned and gave Brian a comrade's slap on the back.

Brian returned the grin, really liking Santiago for the first time. Common danger always created a special fellowship with its own kind of durability and purity.

Santiago moved about the cliff looking for problems. Satisfied there was none, he said, "We arrive in Marseille tomorrow morning. If everything is good we take the boat that night . . . and if it is bad the night that is next." He led Brian to the end of the cliff opposite the lamp post. "I look to the light as a direction to find you here. You have a small light?"

"You mean a flashlight. I have one," Brian said, still completely in the dark about the plan.

"No," Santiago said, changing his mind. "I think it is better to use the light of your motorcycle. It is more large and strong. We will come in a small boat, Brian. I make with the light of the boat two, perhaps three times . . . perhaps more. How many times I make with my light, you with your light make one minus. If I go three times, you light two times. You understand?"

Brian nodded.

"And then I will make again in answer one time minus yours to be certain I am the boat. Yes?"

"That means you will have to signal at least three times to begin."

Santiago worked that over in his mind. "Yes, that is good. If you do not answer me exactly, I will not come to the beach," he instructed with emphasis.

They crossed back to the lamp post where the cliff angled inland, forming one wall of the large ravine that was filled with apartment buildings all the way down to the small beach. Santiago pointed at the beach. "You see the boats." Brian could make out the few rowboats left on the sand during the winter.

Santiago continued confidently, "After the lights you take a boat and come to us. Our boat will come close to the land and then we come with the guns into your boat. Then it is finished," he said, waving triumphantly at the whole world. "Take a boat that is good and goes on the water or . . ." he gave an easy laugh, ". . . or our great *revolución* must swim into *Catalunya*."

"Sounds easy to me," Brian laughed, catching the same humorous feeling.

"*Amigo*." The smile left Santiago's face as he put his arm around

Brian's shoulders. "It will not be that easy. The *Guardia* patrols the roads at night. You must come here before it is dark. What hour we come I do not know. It is a long time and if we not come the first night, you must return each night. We come before the sun if it is to be that night. Sleep in the day."

"Ok."

"Have much clothes. It will be very cold. I give you my big coat I use in the boats. It makes you warm."

"Thanks."

"Is nothing. It is much you have done for us, Brian. If you are discovered with the guns it is not jail like for *la cocaína*. It is the garrote to all in *la revolución*, even a *turista*."

"I know the danger. But like you I must do this. At first, it was only for Nuria. Now it's something I'm doing for all of us. Can you understand there are times you must do something no one can take back?"

"I understand a little of what you say. For me English is difficult in these things. The father of Nuria tells us of the times of *la República*. He tells how there is land for all the peoples, not only the rich. Now it is to begin the dream again."

"Maybe I must do this because I never had a dream like that when I was young," Brian said.

Santiago didn't hear him. He was curled up inside the memories of his own youth. He crossed his arms by grasping his elbows, just like Nuria. "We are crazy perhaps. There are only a few of us and perhaps it will be short. But *Catalunya* will know us. I swear it!"

"Hey!" was the shout from the apartment building behind them.

It startled both of them out of their reverie. "*¿Quí?*" Santiago muttered at the sound.

They could both see a stubby figure waving to them from the doorway of the nearest building.

"It's that American with the loud car . . . George," Brian said when he could make out the approaching figure. How odd his words *that American* sounded to him when he was talking about his own countryman. Perhaps in a small way it meant he did belong to Catalonia.

George held a glass of whisky in one hand and a pistol in the other. When he recognized Brian, he pushed the weapon into the pillow of fat hanging over his belt. "What are you still doing in Tossa?" he asked Brian.

"Just getting ready to leave," Brian answered.

"I thought you'd gone. Your motorcycle wasn't at La Vida," George said suspiciously.

"Just went for a last look around the countryside. Never got to do it last summer."

"What are you two doing out here anyway?" George barked, suddenly nervous about the small talk.

"I wish to show Brian the good *vista*," Santiago said, offering George the same view with his outstretched arm.

George didn't look. He only kept watching the two of them warily.

Santiago took a cautious step toward the motorcycle. "I must be in Tossa soon, Brian."

George let Santiago go a few more steps before he pulled Brian off to the side. "Brian, have you seen my Maria in Tossa?" he asked urgently.

"No," Brian said, backing away from the whisky breath. "Anything wrong?"

"She's been gone two days."

"Why not ask Santiago? He'd know better than me if anything happened in town."

"No," George snapped abruptly. "Can't take the chance . . ." He took a long swallow to kill the rest of his drink. "Brian, I think she was sent to spy on me by the Spanish government."

"That's crazy. What for?"

"You know." George poked Brian's arm for emphasis. "My CIA work here."

"George, that's ridiculous. She's from around here."

"She was a plant. She's gone to tell them. I've got to be ready when they come."

"George . . . I've got to go. Santiago's waiting," Brian said wearily.

"Brian, if anything happens to me . . . call the consulate in Barcelona," George begged as Brian pulled away from his grip. "Tell them the frost has killed Okra."

Brian was almost believing George for the first time since he'd known him. Was it his own recent involvement in intrigue that made it seem possible everyone else was involved too? After all, nobody really knew what George did to make money.

"Remember Okra and tell them about Maria," George pleaded once more to the retreating Brian.

Santiago was still nervous about George's gun. He would not

let Brian start the motorcycle until George had gone inside the apartment.

"You know his woman?" Brian asked, positioning the kick starter.

"I see her at the bus station yesterday. She tells me she goes to her family in Llagostera because the American is always crazy from the whisky."

Santiago was still thoughtfully watching the apartment. He said, "It is bad he is here. I think he is gone when I make this plan. Perhaps it is better to signal from the beach."

"No, he's harmless and besides, it's a good reason for me to be here if the *Guardia* ask," Brian said, standing up over the kick lever.

"*¡Ay!* You are the intelligent one, Brian. You think like the fox," Santiago said, tapping his head.

"All my life," Brian answered back, but his words were lost in the roar of the engine kicking over.

"If it goes bad we meet in Nice at the office of American Express, yes?" Nuria said to Brian.

He nodded and gave another look in the direction the taxi would come. He always hated the waiting during goodbyes. Max was waiting too. It occurred to Brian that when the taxi did leave with Nuria and her cousins, Max would be all that remained of his Tossa world. Judging by his nonchalance, it didn't seem to bother the King of Tossa much.

Nuria lit another cigarette, her third in the few minutes they'd been waiting.

"You two . . . walk," Santiago growled, waving them away. "Marcello and I wait for the taxi."

Brian was glad of the suggestion. Everything he wanted to say seemed better said in private. Halfway down the block, out of earshot, he finally said, "Madeleine knows you are going to Marseille?"

"Yes," was all she answered, self-conscious of her cousins still in sight. They rounded the corner to the church plaza. It was completely deserted during this, the siesta hour. She took a seat on the low wall of the Hostalet terrace.

"Does Madeleine know why you're going?" he asked, boosting himself up on the wall next to her.

"I tell her this morning all that will happen. She only cries. She cries because she lose another to the stupid dream of *Catalunya*. I tell her to no fight is to forget I am Catalan. It is to forget my father and her husband. I am nothing if others fight for what I believe and I do not. But she no does understand. She only cry that the death no does stop in our family."

He couldn't bring himself to take the responsibility of changing her mind, as Madeleine had tried to do. He didn't want her that way anymore. He had to surrender her to the dream, for the sake of the dream. It was always meant to be this way. The hurting was just part of it. He did have to come back from Paris to know it. And accept it.

"You are not angry we never make love."

"No, we have more than that together."

She gave him an uncertain look. The lemon trees behind her looked frail and vulnerable in their winter sparseness.

"Come with us to fight. We will be together," she begged.

"I have no killing left in me. War will kill what we have together. It will make you an animal, too. I am glad I won't be there to see it."

"Why can my mother not understand as you?"

"Maybe she's right. I don't know." He jumped down from the wall. "Come on, the taxi's probably there by now."

"I must do this, Brian."

"I know," he said, as if she were already dead.

When they came around the corner they could see the taxi waiting. Seeing them, Santiago hurried Marcello into the cab before getting in himself. Nuria halted halfway down the block. Her dark eyes gleamed like that first time in the cave.

"Go now," Brian urged. "Go. Goodbyes don't do us any good."

She began walking toward the cab with the feline gait he loved and then, after looking back once, broke into an awkward run. Brian found it hard to even lift his arm for a goodbye wave as she got into the cab.

The taxi ponderously worked its way around the corner and out of sight all too quickly. He stood in the middle of the silent street unable to bring himself to go inside La Vida. He started walking for Bar Simon's, taking the alley shortcut that always gave him the feeling he belonged here. He would keep walking, he told himself, until he had been to all those special places from his summer.

The tobacco shop was opening after the siesta hour. The young girl with the slender nose he knew only by sight was filling up the outside newspaper rack. She gave Brian the noncommittal smile one gives familiar faces in small towns. The gesture buoyed his lonely spirits as he headed toward the beach.

A skeleton of bare awning poles in front of the outdoor cafes and hotels comprised all that remained from the summer scene of tourists and cars. He made his way to the beach. The wind and storms were finally beginning to catch up on the trash left behind. The sand was much cleaner than it had been before he'd gone to Paris. The sea wind cooled his tearing eyes as he saw the longboats and women patiently folding their long green nets. They were all there, of course, because they always would be.

The dawn brought the hills back to life. The boat hadn't arrived from Marseille. Brian's clothes, like everything else, were damp with the morning dew. He stood up from where the grass and weeds were matted down, ready for his return tonight.

He decided to walk the motorcycle back to the main road, even though it meant pushing it up the long service road. But the effort was worth avoiding the risk that the noise of ignition would wake George and create suspicions. He was glad George had been up all night. Listening to the loud music coming from his apartment was all there had been to do to stay awake after the thermos had been emptied. That night he would ration his brandy-laced coffee more judiciously.

Brian was sure the boat would come that night, the second night of waiting. There was no concrete reason for his conviction he would not be returning to Tossa except his own instincts.

The last tinge of blue in the horizon had turned black, bringing on full darkness. Brian could hear no sounds from George's apartment, even though the lights were on. Now that the darkness was complete, the absence of George's music gave the night an uneasy, alien quality. Brian poured himself a stiff measure of the coffee, breaking his carefully planned schedule to make the thermos last until morning. After finishing the ration, there was nothing to do but try to get comfortable and wait.

At first the whine of the tiny Citron engine didn't register on Brian's senses as he was pouring coffee again. Then he whirled from his crouch as the yellow headlights exposed his outpost. The blinding wall of light stopped a few feet away. Doors were opening behind the glare, and he thought he saw two people get out of the car. Still holding the open thermos, he raised his free hand to shade the glare. When the person from the driver's side crossed the no man's land of the headlights, there was no mistake about the outline of the tricornered, patent leather hat and the long lean lines of the rifle.

"*Señor* McCabe." The summons came from the one still behind the yellow lights, on the right-hand side of the car.

Brian still held the thermos as he stood up in answer to his name. There was nothing else to do, with the well-known motorcycle parked next to him.

"It is Raoul." His voice was generous with friendship. "What do you do here?"

"I came to visit my friend there." Brian pointed to the light in George's apartment. "But the sea looked too beautiful to miss before going inside."

"I didn't know you were such good friends with George."

Raoul passed through the lights. "What have you there?" he asked, bending slightly over the mouth of the thermos in Brian's hand to catch the aroma. "You bring your own drinks to the house of a friend?"

"The ride gets cold."

"*Señor* McCabe," Raoul gave out a toying laugh. "You should have stayed in town and come to see me. We could have played that game of chess we spoke of."

"We're having it right now," Brian said with a grin, eyeing the other *Guardia* soldier moving over to the edge of the cliff.

Raoul grew somber. "*Señor* McCabe." He took a pack of cigarettes from his pocket. "I know why you are here. Today, Nuria's mother came to my office. You had left Tossa and we could not find you until I realized this is the only place nearby to land a boat."

Brian refused the offer of a cigarette. The old Zippo lighter Raoul used to light his own cigarette seemed to stir a sentimental memory. He said absentmindedly, "Paul gave me this as a gift his first year in Tossa. It still works. The best invention in America, I think."

Raoul took a long drag on the cigarette. "I know about the guns, the cousins too," he said, changing to a businesslike tone. "Madeleine said you were to meet Nuria with the guns."

"I don't know what you're talking about."

"*Señor* McCabe." Raoul's voice was losing its friendly tone. "*Señora* Madeleine did not come to me because she is loyal to my government. She comes because she is afraid that Nuria will die in this ridiculous joke. I have assured her if we take the guns now the only charge could be smuggling. I will do everything I can to minimize the crimes."

"Raoul, I don't know what this is about; and if I did, it seems you don't need me since you have all the information."

"*Señor* McCabe, the information I need is how they intend to land the guns. I told you once that I never see anyone three times in my office, you remember?"

Brian didn't bother to answer. He was sneaking another quick glance at the guard who was very nervous. Tonight wasn't the usual safe, dreary winter patrol of a fishing village.

"*Señor* McCabe," Raoul said in a louder voice to get Brian's attention, "Nuria will be arrested without your help. A patrol boat is on the way from Barcelona. I imagine you are here because there is a signal. If you tell me the signal, then no one will be hurt. You may take your motorcycle and leave. There will be no charges against you if you assure me you are leaving Spain and will not return."

"I really don't know what you're talking about."

"Do not be insulting." Raoul threw his cigarette away in disgust. "What is gained by not telling me the signal? Only a very long, and I assure you, unpleasant time in a Spanish prison. Neither my government nor yours wishes the publicity of an American helping a revolution. You can be certain I am telling the truth. If you tell me the signal, as soon as they come to land you are free to go. You need not stay to see them."

"If it's against the law for me to be here, say so and I will leave," Brian argued as a stall while he thought all this out. His words came out a little too fast, betraying his own fear.

He shifted his weight so he could turn more to the north where he expected the boat. Raoul's unconscious countermove put the sea at his back. Brian realized they hadn't connected any of this with the agent's killing. That's why Raoul could be so generous as to let him go. He thought he could barely hear the putter of a small engine coming from the north. In the dim reflected light of the new moon, nothing was visible. Instinctively, though, he knew it was Nuria's boat. If he did not give a return signal they would run. The patrol boat had not arrived yet, so they would get away. He would go free too, without any evidence yet collected.

"You are not betraying them," Raoul pleaded. Frustrated anger had replaced his impatience. "Do not be a complete fool. It is finished no matter what you do. Help me and you go free. *¡Por Dios!* Brian, you are too young to pay this much of a price. You are doing this for nothing. Nuria as a woman will perhaps not even go to jail."

"And Marcello and Santiago?"

"A few years in prison. I make no promises."

What Raoul said made sense. Everything Brian knew about Raoul said he could be trusted. All Brian had to do was tell him to flash the light one less time, and he could leave as the boat came into the cove. He could walk over to the bike and head for France. Why not? He'd tried as much as he could for these people, given up more than anyone could expect. He would be saving them from everything he hated. Now he could hear the larger motor of the patrol boat coming from the south. It was surely all over now, so why not tell Raoul and at least get himself out of this? Nothing could save the others.

The guard said something to Raoul.

"I will let you leave," Raoul repeated, sensing Brian's thoughts.

"Yes, I believe you."

"Then tell me how to stop this foolishness."

"I can't, Raoul."

"Why not?" The begging tone had assumed a priority in the commander's voice.

"I don't know how to explain it. Paul may know. You'll have to ask him some time."

"Brian, we will stop the boat, no matter; my guard has said the patrol boat is here. The first boat to come too near the beach will be stopped."

Brian tried to remember how far sound travels over water. A shot from Raoul's pistol was the only way to warn them before the patrol boat got too close. They would run at the sound of the shot, and the faster patrol boat would eventually catch them; but if Santiago were thinking, he would already have dumped the guns into the sea. With no evidence aboard, they would be in the clear.

But getting to Raoul's pistol, which was still in the holster, meant quick and desperate action, maybe even killing; and Brian didn't have any more killing in him. He could jump Raoul, but the guard with the rifle, to avoid shooting Raoul by mistake, would probably club Brian before he could even get the pistol out of the holster. . . . Or he could go for the guard on the cliff instead. . . . He just knew he had to do something, anything but stand there and merely await the inevitable.

Suddenly Brian hurled his thermos over the cliff. The movement made Raoul instinctively reach for his gun. The guard turned to follow the trajectory of the thermos, giving Brian the split-second chance to maneuver Raoul between himself and the guard.

"That will warn no one," Raoul said as he pulled out his pistol in absentminded readiness. The pistol was Brian's bait for action. He still didn't know exactly what he was going to do as he moved toward the pistol. But there was no doubt this first step would be the most irrevocable act of his life.

Out of the corner of his eye he thought he saw George duck away from his window. After all his CIA talk, George was running to hide under the bed, Brian grimly joked to himself.

"Brian, *basta!* Stop!" Raoul's pistol pointed stiffly at point blank range.

"Raoul, you are going to have to shoot me. I will not stop." Brian could see the guard angling for a clear shot from where he stood because there was no time to move.

"I don't want to shoot you!" Raoul waved the gun helplessly.

Brian grabbed for the pistol. He braced himself for the shot, but Raoul's eyes told him it wouldn't come. The cold barrel slipped out of his grasp, but Brian knew it was the useless part of the prize anyway. He had to control the trigger! Only the shot mattered, not the aim. Raoul's body was squirming inside his arms, trying to push Brian off balance. The old man was stronger than he looked.

Brian let go long enough with one hand to try for the gun again. He didn't have to wrest it away. He needed only to make Raoul's finger squeeze the trigger. He caught the oily-feeling barrel again, then let go, instead pinning Raoul in a bear hug as they moved even closer to the cliff's edge. The slow beat of the surf rose up from below. Would there be a scream as one of them fell? Would it be loud enough to be heard on the boat that far away?

Raoul freed his gun hand from between their bodies, pointing the pistol skyward in front of Brian's face. Before Brian could act, it had sailed out past his eyes into the sea.

This was the one possibility Brian had not considered. "Why didn't you shoot me?" he cried.

The eyes of the old soldier blinked with a terminal weariness. Brian shoved the deflated man to the ground. The guard's elbow twitched as he prepared to squeeze the trigger.

"No," Raoul protested, rising to one knee. "*¡No lo mate!*"

The guard froze, obeying the order.

Brian moved toward the rifleman. They would have to shoot; he would die. He knew he had to die even now, when there was no reason for it. The guard retreated with a quick glance at the lip of the cliff and then stopped. He had run out of steps to avoid Brian.

"No lo mate," Raoul kept repeating. Brian now had the guard trapped against the cliff. He would have to shoot in self-defense. The guard wouldn't want to die on account of orders. No one wanted to die, not even Brian, yet he began the last imponderable step. It was like wading through quicksand.

At first, the flash and loud crack exploding the silence seemed remote to Brian. The rifle pointing at him had whirled toward some new, more pressing menace. More distant flashes were followed by pops crackling like firecrackers.

"Run, Brian!" George shouted, as he hurtled down the sidewalk, pistol in hand. "They've broken my cover! Run!"

The nearby rifle flared with a deafening boom in Brian's ear, severing the strings of the charging marionette. The guard held his disciplined firing position on the crumpling target until, too late, he remembered Brian standing next to him.

He had only half-turned the rifle when Brian's cross-body block sent him over the cliff uttering a life-draining scream. . . .

As Brian turned on Raoul, he could have sworn he heard a woman call out to him from the sea. Raoul instinctively reached for his empty holster before realizing the gun was gone. The mistake gave Brian a momentary advantage to move before Raoul could set himself aright as he rose from his knees. Brian got behind Raoul, whipping his arm across the old man's windpipe. He pressed his wrist against the Adam's apple until he felt the man's struggles slacken. Then he let Raoul drop to the ground, leaving him to his helpless, spasmodic vomiting.

Brian dashed to his motorcycle. He pushed the electric starter, hoping there was enough power for one start. The engine cranked sympathetically and then roared to life. Brian wrestled the machine around in the dirt, brushing off Raoul's last weak attempt to stop him.

He raced past the dark wall of houses, the hateful growl of the motorcycle betraying his position. He could see no guards where he expected them to be each time the road turned. Even the entrance to the housing development was empty. Miraculously, he was escaping from yet another jungle. They must've heard the shots on the boat, so they'd be running for France, too.

Something inexplicable made Brian turn in the direction of Tossa—not the border. The motorcycle hurtled up the coastal road without challenge. Through the tunnel the roar of the engine was deafening, so Brian never heard the shot. He watched the road careening up at him like a huge breaking wave as the motorcycle slipped away from between his legs, and he was thrown forever against the enduring green hills.

L'Hivern

L'HIVERN
(Winter)

Curiosity and concern would not let me pass through Barcelona without trying to reach Brian before I continued on my way to the Canaries for Christmas like I'd planned. There had been no answer each time I'd phoned La Vida, which could've meant he'd left Tossa; but I had to know for sure. Phoning Raoul to see if everything was all right didn't seem like such a good idea. Calling out of the blue might raise unnecessary suspicions. So I decided to take the bus to Tossa for the day.

Barcelona was too big for a little incident like the killing of an American to be much news; but in Tossa, of course, everyone knew about it. By the time I'd walked from the bus station to La Vida, I had an idea of what happened. The fate of Nuria and her cousins differed with each version, but there was no doubt Brian was dead. Outwardly, I showed shock and dismay to each person telling me my friend was dead, but I felt a kind of tranquilizing sense of relief it was finally over, as if I'd always known somewhere deep down that it had to end like this; that it had only been a matter of time.

It didn't take Raoul long to hear I was in town and track me down at La Vida. He seemed to have aged years in the month I'd been gone. He told me Nuria and her cousins had tried to make a run for it, but the boat suddenly exploded, probably caused by a stray shot from the pursuing patrol boat. They never found Nuria's body, only the others. Raoul wanted to believe she'd jumped overboard and gotten away. Her body could just as easily have washed out to sea, but I didn't offer that possibility because he seemed to need so much to believe Nuria was still alive. Either way, by this time the truth about Nuria didn't matter to me. Wasn't it all just a crock of shit anyway, now that it was over?

"You know your friend is dead, too," Raoul said, finally getting around to it.

"It was the first thing I heard when I got off the bus."

"I am sorry, Pablo. He left no choice."

"It had to be this way."

"I was there when it happened, Pablo."

"I don't want to know about it," I said, feeling the tension build inside me. "It doesn't do anyone any good now."

"It is important to me you know I did not kill him. I could not do it even when it was my duty, and one of my men died because of my cowardice."

For a moment Raoul couldn't seem to go on with what he still had to say. Then he said, "Pablo, they wish you to leave. You remember after they were in jail last summer, I said trouble for Brian was trouble for you. The mayor wants it this way."

"Would it matter if I said he was not my friend?"

"Perhaps." Raoul's voice rose with hope. "I could speak to the mayor, tell him you knew nothing of all this . . ." he went on, thinking out the whole story. "I would stand up for you. My friends in Gerona could help. I'm sure I can persuade them to let you stay in Tossa, even keep La Vida . . ."

"Forget it, Raoul," I cut in. "He was my friend."

I couldn't have lived with myself if I'd told the mayor or anyone else anything different. I couldn't betray Brian's existence, even for the sake of my summers in Tossa. It was the distance I felt between me and other people. It had always been there, but when I was young I knew I still had the coming years. The future always seemed time enough to face up to myself and gain a foothold. Now, I'd run out of time when it didn't hurt to be alone. I just couldn't deny Brian this time. I couldn't be that *alone*.

There was still plenty of daylight left on that December day when I told Raoul I wanted to take a final walk by myself. The last request of the condemned man, you might say. A woman at her door in a yellow robe made me think of Claude still back in Paris and never hearing from any of us. She, more than anyone else, deserved to know what had happened.

I went to the post office to send her a telegram, but how do you really say all those terrible words?

CLAUDE

BRIAN WILL NOT BE COMING BACK TO ANY OF US. EVER. IF IT HELPS YOUR SADNESS I WANT YOU TO KNOW I THINK

THE ONLY ONE HE WOULD HAVE COME BACK TO IS YOU. AM LEAVING TOSSA FOR GOOD TOO. LETTER COMING WITH DETAILS.

PAUL

I went out past the bus station for a last look at the Roman ruins. Tossa's pride and joy attraction for the tourists is really nothing that special, just a few bits and pieces of the floor and walls of an old Roman house. Looking at the old stones, I was thinking maybe Brian's irrevocable act wasn't so epic, either—really very ordinary in that he was just another dude like the rest of us trying to believe in something. . . .

But how do I believe in anything, when all I've built in nine years had just been crumpled up and casually thrown away like a scrap of worthless paper?

I walked faster, suddenly wanting this little stroll to be over. Actually, there was nobody or nothing I really wanted to see. Imagine that, after living nine years in Tossa! I told myself it was because this wasn't the freak Tossa I'd always talked about. This was off-season Tossa. But now I find myself wondering how really wonderful summer in Tossa was. Can anything be so wonderful if it leaves you this empty and useless when it's over?

There was nothing to do but wait for Raoul to take me to the boat, so I kept on walking until I found myself standing in front of the Llibertat. Maybe I'd subconsciously ended up there because Madeleine was the only other person left in Tossa who was a part of my life. I tried the handle on the door, halfway hoping it would be locked so I could go away without facing her. The latch was off and the warped door shivered against the jamb when I pushed it open.

The bar was as fresh and clear as spring water in the daylight. It was a different world than the nighttime Llibertat in which I'd spent all those hours. The delicate curve of the bartop, the half-moon archway and all the other round shapes of the bottles and glasses that had dominated the room in the orange night light now gave way to the straight lines of the walls and tables and chairs.

Madeleine's footsteps were almost soundless on the stairs as she came to see who it was. Despite everything she still had a majestic bearing. "The bar is closed," she told me in Spanish.

"I didn't come for a drink. I am here to offer my condolences for your tragedy."

"You lost a friend, also."

Her matching sympathy loosened up my awkwardness. "Madeleine, Raoul said you are the one who told him. Why? I have to know why."

"There is no reason I should tell you," she said cautiously, and took her regular stool at the bar as an added defense.

"We both lost people we cared about."

"And lovers?"

"Brian said they were never lovers, if that's any comfort to you."

"I know. I said *we* both lost lovers." She went on like she thought I knew everything. "Her own daughter, you are thinking. Why her own daughter? I wanted to protect her from the guns and the death. There has been too much war in my life. Perhaps that is not all of it. Yes, a part of me was jealous when she was with your American. Raoul said she would not be in jail long. We would have been together again, and your friend would have had to leave Spain forever."

She put her head between her hands, letting out a soft sob. "I did not know it would end like this, but my terror is I would still do the same thing, even knowing it. She and her father are all I have."

Crazy thoughts of incest and lesbianism came to mind, but I didn't pursue it. What sense was there in going into such things now? I sat on the stool next to her, as if we were travelling companions taking the same journey. She understood that sameness, and gave me a grateful smile.

All that time I was using up my Tossa summers playing silly games when a real woman was right there with needs and hurts that had peeled away over the years until there was only this nightmare left for both of us. Maybe we could've helped each other. And then again, maybe this was only a momentary fantasy on my part because I knew I was leaving and would never see her again. I could run from the edge this time, too!

"The mayor has closed my bar. I am leaving Tossa forever," I said.

"We have both lost everything from my action. I am leaving Tossa also. Now there is no reason for me to remain here. All of my Catalonia is dead."

"I missed out, Madeleine. Maybe we both did . . . and I'm angry about it now, when it is too late."

"If you are angry, it is never too late."

The King of Tossa was there to see me off this last time, like all the other times I'd left Tossa. He was watching me from behind the mask of black fur that gave his eyes their resolute sense of endurance. I gave Max an extra-special goodbye pat on the head, saying, *"Ave Caesar, morituri te salutamus."* Raoul, who had been waiting for me patiently at the wheel of his car, struggled with a consoling smile, pretending he understood what I'd meant. But I could see he really didn't understand at all what made Max so special: Max would outlast all of us because he knew the secret of Tossa better than anyone, even me.

You'd see the new strays in town for two, maybe three months, and then one day they're gone. They just disappear without having been around long enough to get a name from the residents. But Max's something else again. He's been at it for more than nine years now because he never broke the rules of summer . . . never let himself care like I did this one time. That's why he's still the King, the leader of the pack of all the Tossa strays.

As the distance widens between Brian and me with each turn of the ship's engines, I'm more aware of how alike we were; not because of the aimless summer drift of our solitary lives or these events that forced us both to the brink of decision, but because I'm battered by all the very same fears that stalked him. They were in me, too, all along, only buried deeper. Now at last they've forced their way to the surface, and somehow it all feels better.

That last time I saw him on the street corner in Paris, I was feeling so apart. I was so envious because he'd found for himself what we all wanted. And at the same time I was so happy for him. I was happy because . . . because . . . yes, I can say the words now . . . because I loved him!

THE END

EPILOGUE

November 20, 1975: General Francisco Franco died of natural causes.

November 22, 1975: Juan Carlos de Borbón y Borbón was proclaimed King of Spain.

September 29, 1977: The Spanish Government restored the ancient Catalan home rule body called the Generalitat to administer the four Catalan provinces of Barcelona, Gerona, Lerida, and Tarragona with limited self-governing authority.

Printed March 1979 for Dryad Press by
Mackintosh & Young. Design and
typography by Graham Mackintosh. This
edition is limited to 1000 copies, of which
100 have been handbound in boards by
Linda Benet and numbered and signed by
the author.